GHOST TOWNS

of the

AMERICAN WEST

Bill O'Neal

Publications International, Ltd.

Bill O'Neal's eleven book credits include *Legends of the Wild West, Encyclopedia of Western Gunfighters, Henry Brown: The Outlaw Marshal, The Arizona Rangers,* and *Fighting Men of the Indian Wars.* He is a member of the Western Writers of America, Inc., a past president of the East Texas Historical Association, and a board member of the National Association for Outlaw and Lawman History. He has been a member of the history department of Panola Junior College since 1970.

Editorial Assistant: **M. David Key**

Photo Credits

Front cover: **Dick Dietrich/FPG International.**

Back cover: **Dick Dietrich.**

Courtesy Department of Library Services, American Museum of Natural History: 31 (top); **AP/Wide World Photos:** 119, 167 (bottom), 238; **Appel Color Photography:** 251; **Archive Photos:** 134; American Stock: 165 (top right, top center & bottom right); Hirz: 149; Emil Muench: 261 (bottom); **Arizona Historical Society, Tucson:** 99 (top right), 198 (left); **Steven Astillero/Nature's Design Photography:** 302, 303, 304, 305 (bottom), 306, 308, 309 (bottom); **Noella Ballenger:** 240, 242 (top right & bottom right), 261 (top), 264 (bottom); Tulley/Ballenger: 265; **Ron Behrmann:** 183, 189, 197 (top), 207; **Bettmann Archive:** 12, 14, 15, 21 (left), 23, 120 (left), 125, 165 (bottom left), 198 (bottom right), 199, 213 (top left), 231, 236, 241; **Steve Bly:** 18, 20 (bottom), 274-275, 281, 284, 285, 290, 291, 292, 293; **D&R Bretzfelder:** 107, 115 (bottom), 155, 157; **Jan Butchofsky-Houser:** 20 (top), 172 (center), 215 (top right), 264 (top); **Cal Farley's Boys Ranch:** 58 (right), 59 (top); **Carson County Square House Museum, Panhandle, Texas:** 56 (left); **Jeanette Cartie:** 132, 133, 136, 137, 138; **Central Nevada Museum:** 224, 225, 226; **Lynne Clark Collection:** 252; **Colorado Historical Society:** 86 (bottom), 88 (bottom), 95, 99 (bottom left & bottom right), 100, 108, 110, 111 (top right & bottom right), 115 (top), 118 (top), 120 (right); Collection of Fred M. Mazzulla: 121 (bottom left); **Denver Public Library, Western History Department:** End sheets, 17, 86 (top), 87, 88 (top), 89, 96,

121 (top left), 129 (top); **Dickinson Press:** 24, 29; **Dick Dietrich:** 9 (bottom), 162, 163, 164, 170 (bottom), 171; **Terry Donnelly:** 102-103; **Jim Edwards:** 32, 33, 38 (bottom), 42, 43; **Gary Elam:** 244, 245, 248, 249; **John Elkins:** 124 (left); **FPG International:** 257, 260; Dave Bartruff: 19 (bottom); Tom Carroll: 218 (right); Peter Gridley: 13; Spencer Jones: 256; Lee Kuhn: 173 (top), 160-161; David Noble: 22, 131; Travelpix: 9 (top), 84, 85, 90, 91 (top left), 97, 211, 218 (left), 220-221; Union Pacific Railroad: 109; **Richard Frederick:** 294, 295, 299 (bottom left & bottom right), 300; **Jim Galli:** 222, 223, 229, 232, 233, 234, 235, 242 (left); **David Hiser/Photographers Aspen:** 101 (bottom left & bottom right), 104, 253, 254, 276; **Robert Holmes:** 262-263; **Janaloo Hill Hough Collection:** 184, 185 (bottom); **Dave G. Houser:** 8 (bottom), 19 (top), 21 (right), 112 (bottom), 113, 114, 121 (right), 123 (left), 140, 144 (top), 145 (bottom left), 159, 190, 196, 197 (bottom), 200, 213 (top right & bottom); **Idaho State Historical Society:** 279, 280, 282 (top), 286, 288, 289; **Kerrick James:** 8 (top), 170 (top), 210, 216, 217, 219, 267; **Kansas State Historical Society, Topeka, Kansas:** 34, 35, 36 (bottom), 37 (top & bottom), 38 (top), 39 (top), 40, 41, 193 (center & bottom); **Susan Kaye:** 123 (right); **James Kidd:** 172 (top), 182, 186, 188 (top); **Jeanne Kidd:** 167 (top), 169, 174, 175, 178, 179, 181; **Library of Congress:** 118 (bottom), 212, 239; **Robert and Linda Mitchell:** 74, 75, 79, 80, 81; **Montana Historical Society:** 142, 143, 144 (bottom), 152, 153, 154; **Ray Morris:** 44, 45, 47 (top), 48 (right), 49 (top), 52, 53; **Robert Mulherin:** 54, 55, 59 (left), 62, 64, 65, 67, 70, 71, 72, 73 (left), **Museum of New Mexico:** 193 (top), 194, 195 (top), 205; **National Archives/Lincoln County Heritage Trust:** 185 (top); **Nevada Historical Society:** 227; **Rio Grande Historical Collections/Hobson-Huntsinger University Archives, New Mexico State University Library:** 206; **Old Mobeetie Texas Association Jail Museum, Mobeetie, Texas:** 69; **Jack Olson:** 25 (bottom), 31 (bottom), 91 (top right), 94, 101 (top left & right), 105 (top), 111 (left), 122, 124 (right), 145 (bottom right), 148 (top), 172 (bottom), 195 (bottom), 215 (top left); **Oregon Historical Society:** 305 (top), 309 (top); **Panhandle-Plains His-**

torical Museum, Canyon, Texas: 56 (right), 57 (top & bottom), 58 (left), 60, 61, 63, 66, 68; **Laurence Parent:** 6, 10-11, 78, 82-83, 92-93, 191, 201, 202, 203, 208-209; **Radeka/SuperStock:** 266, 269 (top), 273; **John Reddy:** 145 (top), 146; **J. R. Riddle/Museum of New Mexico:** 192; **Sam Houston Memorial Museum, Huntsville, Texas:** 73 (right); **Sharlot Hall Museum Library/Archives, Prescott, Arizona:** 166; **James C. Simmons:** 269 (bottom), 272; **Friends of South Pass, South Pass City State Historic Site:** 128; Tibbal Collection: 129 (bottom); **Southern Oregon Historical Society:** 307; **State Historical Society of North Dakota:** 25 (top), 27, 28, 30; **Jim Steinberg:** 91 (bottom), 105 (bottom), 106, 112 (top), 116, 230; **Archives of the Big Bend, Bryan Wildenthal Memorial Library, Sul Ross State University, Alpine, Texas:** 77; **SuperStock:** 117, 126, 127, 130, 141, 148 (bottom), 150, 151, 156, 158, 187, 188 (bottom), 215 (bottom right), 268, 277, 282 (bottom), 283; **Hugh Tessendorf:** 36 (top), 39 (bottom); **Transcendental Graphics:** 198 (top right); **Travel Montana:** 147; **Courtesy Special Publications, University of Arizona Library:** 176-177, 180; **University of Nevada, Las Vegas Library:** Courtesy of Edwards Collection: 215 (bottom left); Courtesy of Nye County Collection: 247 (bottom); Courtesy of Single Item Accessions Collection: 246, 247 (top); Courtesy of Squires Collection: 228 (bottom); Courtesy of Tonopah-Goldfield Collection: 228 (top); **Western History Collections, University of Oklahoma Library:** 46, 47 (bottom), 48 (left), 49 (bottom), 50, 51, 99 (top left), 165 (top left), 168, 173 (bottom); **Special Collections Division, University of Washington Libraries:** 296 (top), 299 (top); **American Heritage Center, University of Wyoming:** 135, 139 (top), 258, 259; **The Virginian, by Owen Wister; cover illustration from a painting by Frederic Remington, Courtesy of Amon Carter Museum, Forth Worth, Texas; Gramercy Books, New York, 1995:** 139 (bottom); **Washington County Historical Society:** Leroy Radanovich Collection: 270, (bottom left), 271; Zora Wommack Collection: 270 (top right); **Washington State Historical Society, Tacoma:** 296 (bottom), 297, 301; **LuWayne Wood:** 250, 255.

Contents

Abandoned home in Terlingua, Texas.

Mine buildings in Creede, Colorado.

6 Introduction

10 The Middle West

12 Deadwood, South Dakota

24 Medora, North Dakota

32 Caldwell, Kansas

44 Ingalls, Oklahoma

54 Tascosa, Texas

66 Mobeetie, Texas

74 Terlingua, Texas

82 The Rocky Mountains

84 Cripple Creek, Colorado

96 Leadville, Colorado

106 Central City, Colorado

116 Creede, Colorado

126 South Pass City, Wyoming

132 Medicine Bow, Wyoming

140 Virginia City, Montana

150 Bannack, Montana

The Southwest 160

Tombstone, Arizona 162

Silverbell, Arizona 174

Shakespeare, New Mexico 182

Lincoln, New Mexico 190

White Oaks, New Mexico 202

Virginia City, Nevada 210

Tonopah, Nevada 222

Goldfield, Nevada 234

Aurora, Nevada 244

Grafton, Utah 250

Bodie, California 256

Hornitos, California 268

The Northwest 274

Silver City, Idaho 276

Idaho City, Idaho 284

Port Blakely, Washington 294

Jacksonville, Oregon 302

Index 310

Cattle grazing outside Bodie, California.

Main Street in Silver City, Idaho.

Introduction

I nearly swooned when I saw my first Western ghost town. Throughout boyhood, I had viewed Western movies with ghost town scenes and enjoyed Western novels set in deserted frontier communities. As an adolescent, I pored through Lambert Florin's captivating series of ghost town books, examining his photos through a magnifying glass and tracing the location of one decaying town after another in an old atlas.

In November of 1963, during the Thanksgiving holiday of my senior year in college, I ventured into the Big Bend area of Texas, accompanied by

Crumbling house in Terlingua, Texas.

my friend and mentor, Cecil Williams. We traveled to Terlingua, generally considered the best ghost town in Texas, where we explored crumbling rock houses, the old Catholic church and rectory, collapsed mine shafts, a decaying adobe school, a tiny jail, and a quaint *cemeterio*, all surrounded by a barren but majestic desert.

The abandoned company headquarters—a two-story adobe structure perched atop a windy hill—featured an open dining area on the top floor. Noting, for no apparent reason, that there was plenty of room for dancing, I suddenly imagined a dancing partner in a beautiful Victorian dress. It was my first ghost town, and my imagination soared. For the first time in my life, I had experienced the nostalgic thrill of prowling the streets and buildings of the 19th century. I was hooked!

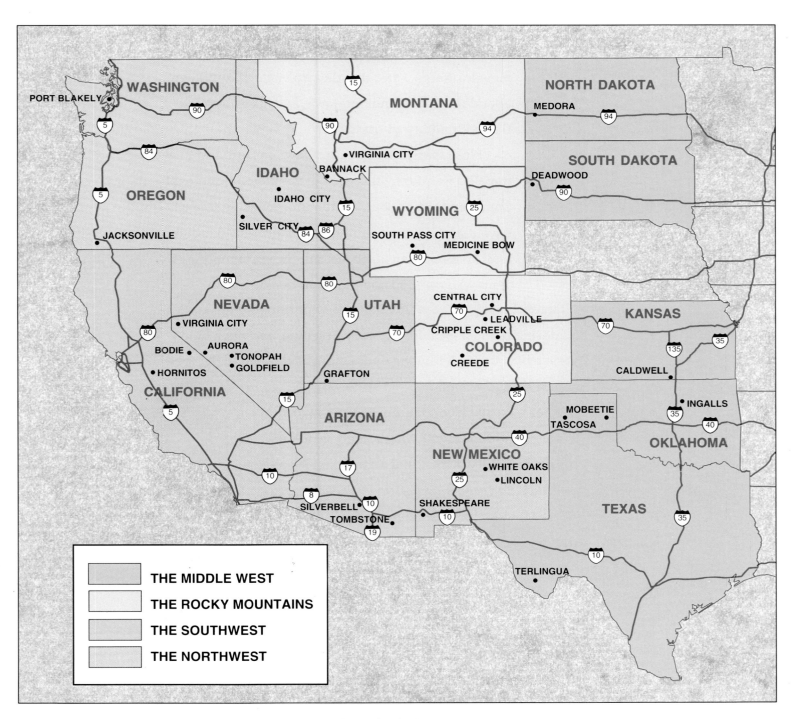

WASHINGTON

PORT BLAKELY

MONTANA

NORTH DAKOTA

MEDORA

OREGON

IDAHO

VIRGINIA CITY
BANNACK

IDAHO CITY

SOUTH DAKOTA

DEADWOOD

SILVER CITY

JACKSONVILLE

WYOMING

SOUTH PASS CITY
MEDICINE BOW

NEVADA

UTAH

CENTRAL CITY

KANSAS

VIRGINIA CITY

LEADVILLE

BODIE
HORNITOS

AURORA
TONOPAH
GOLDFIELD

GRAFTON

CRIPPLE CREEK

COLORADO

CREEDE

CALDWELL

CALIFORNIA

INGALLS

ARIZONA

MOBEETIE
TASCOSA

NEW MEXICO

WHITE OAKS
LINCOLN

OKLAHOMA

SILVERBELL
TOMBSTONE

SHAKESPEARE

TEXAS

TERLINGUA

THE MIDDLE WEST

THE ROCKY MOUNTAINS

THE SOUTHWEST

THE NORTHWEST

Regional map shows the approximate locations of the ghost towns featured in this book.

Ruins of Standard Mine in Bodie.

Our next stop, just a few miles away, was Study Butte, a smaller mining ruin distinguished by its tall elevator frame. Later that day we visited Shafter, an abandoned silver-mining town, and sprawling Fort Davis, a military ghost town.

More than three decades have passed, and I have traveled frequently throughout the West, taking every opportunity to encounter frontier ghosts. At times I have had the company of my wife, my four daughters, and, on more than 20 occasions, groups of college students who camped and explored beside me.

I have witnessed many of these adventurers experiencing the special thrill of encountering a ghost town for the very first time, and each time I visit a new ghost town I can still feel the excitement of walking in the footsteps of pioneer men and women.

What qualifies a Western community as a ghost town? Obviously, an abandoned town with dilapidated structures and an overgrown cemetery is the ideal destination for a genuine ghost town buff. Bodie, California, and Bannack, Montana, deserted except for a few state park employees, offer numerous venerable buildings in wonderfully isolated settings. But such towns are increasingly rare, because abandoned structures eventually deteriorate and collapse, or are destroyed by fire, or are moved to another location. Sometimes they are dismantled for their materials.

Abandoned buildings in Bodie.

A number of ghost towns, such as Shakespeare, New Mexico, and Mobeetie, Texas, still host a few inhabitants. Historic Lincoln, New Mexico, is likewise home to a small number of permanent residents.

Most of the old buildings remain intact, and Billy the Kid and his cronies would probably feel right at home were they to reappear there today.

Similarly, long departed Tascosans would probably recognize the Texas town's original school and courthouse—and Boot Hill, which they helped develop—even though the remainder of the town site is covered with new streets and the modern buildings of Cal Farley's Boys Ranch.

Several other famous towns—including Tombstone, Arizona; Cripple Creek, Colorado; Goldfield, Nevada; Leadville, Colorado; and both Virginia Cities (Nevada and Montana)—retain substantial populations, primarily to accommodate tourists. In each community, however, the number of residents today is only a fraction of the population during its frontier heyday.

Downtown Cripple Creek, Colorado.

Another type of ghost town is exemplified by Caldwell, Kansas. Once the wildest town on the Chisholm Trail, Caldwell today has about the same population (1,500)—if none of the same orneriness—it had a century ago. Many 19th-century buildings still stand in the quiet farm town, and a walk through its streets makes its historic past come alive. Walking, of course, is the best way to experience any ghost town.

Whether you end up wandering alone among the few remaining structures of an abandoned mining camp or negotiating crowded streets filled with tourists and souvenir shops, if the place is "haunted" you'll feel it. That, as much as anything else, is what defines a genuine ghost town.

Bill O'Neal

Bill O'Neal

Carthage, Texas

Tombstone's Boot Hill.

THE MIDDLE WEST

DEADWOOD
SOUTH DAKOTA

As early as the 1830s, Indian legends about gold brought prospectors to South Dakota's Black Hills. The region was considered holy ground by the Sioux, however, and small groups of prospectors were in constant danger of attack.

In 1868, the Black Hills were ceded by treaty to the Sioux, barring white settlement permanently. Six years later, Lieutenant Colonel George Armstrong Custer and his 7th Cavalry arrived to locate a site for a fort, and "gold in paying quantities" was discovered by two men accompanying the expedition. Prospectors immediately swarmed into the area, triggering a war that would climax with Custer's death and end with the final subjugation of the Sioux.

In August of 1875, seven prospectors set up a camp on Whitewood Creek near the future site of Deadwood. Discouraged, they moved their camp within a few

View of Deadwood in 1888, nine years after fire destroyed most of the business district. The thriving mining town rebuilt quickly—and continued to expand.

Downtown Deadwood today is almost as busy as it was in the 1870s, with tourists thronging the old town's new casinos.

days, but in November, Frank Bryant returned and found gold just east of the log cabin his party had built a few months earlier. When news of the strike spread, thousands of claims were staked out along Whitewood, Deadwood, Gold Run, Blacktail, and other area creeks.

A tent city quickly went up along Deadwood Gulch. The first building to go up was V. C. Gardner's grocery store. Throughout 1876, one structure after another was erected on the floor of the narrow gulch. Eventually, there were more saloons and dance halls than stores. By the time the Grand Central Hotel was finished, a telegraph line had been strung to the outside world and upward of 20,000 men surged into the area.

Prospectors panned for gold and ran sluice boxes along Deadwood Creek and other nearby streams. The muddy main street was filled with men and horses, mule- and ox-drawn wagons, and huge piles of lumber for the frenzy of construction projects. The Chinese laundries, restaurants, and import shops in the lower end of the gulch soon came to be known as Chinatown.

Wild Bill Hickok was the most famous of a stream of frontier notables who gravitated to the West's newest boomtown. Wild Bill and two

Right: Mathew Brady portrait of George Armstrong Custer. **Far right:** During the 1874 Black Hills Expedition, Custer's 1,000-man column enjoyed baseball games, community sings, hunting, and fishing. An avid hunter, Custer (center) fulfilled his dream of bagging a grizzly bear.

Deadwood's busy Main Street in 1876. The frontier town was less than a year old when this photo was taken, its rapid growth fueled by the discovery of gold in the surrounding hills.

friends set up a tent, the most common accommodation, and Hickok was soon invited to make Number 10 Saloon his gambling headquarters. Wyatt and Morgan Earp turned up, as did Calamity Jane and a young Texas cowboy named Sam Bass.

Bass and Joel Collins drove a cattle herd to Deadwood, operated a freight line and a saloon for a time, then went broke on a mining venture. The two men thereupon enlisted several eager desperadoes and systematically robbed seven stagecoaches before leaving the Black Hills for criminal activities in Texas.

In addition to robberies and claim-jumping, there were numerous shootouts. In one such episode, Turkey Creek Jack Johnson quarreled with his two mining partners in a Deadwood saloon. The three men marched out to the cemetery, followed by a large crowd of spectators. At a considerable distance the two partners opened fire and grazed Johnson, who coolly shot them dead. Johnson paid for the burials, but the graves had to be blasted out of the frozen ground with dynamite.

Deadwood's first newspaper, the *Black Hills Pioneer,* ran the following editorial on July 13, 1876: "Anyone who has been here for a space of a week and has witnessed the shootings, robbings, and brawls that enliven our nights and interrupt our days must realize that it is high time that some form of recognized law be established in Deadwood City."

A couple of weeks later, one of the most infamous shootings in Western history occurred in the Number 10 Saloon when Wild Bill Hickok was murdered by Jack McCall. The killer, who owed Hickok $110 and who may have been hired to assassinate the famous gunfighter, caught Wild Bill off guard, seated with his back to the room.

After blasting Wild Bill with the only good cartridge in his .45 (all other rounds proved defective), McCall was captured, tried, and acquitted. But no formal legal system existed in Deadwood, and McCall was retried before the federal court in Yankton. Convicted and sentenced to hang on March 1, 1877, McCall was asked, "Why didn't you go around in front of Wild Bill and shoot him like a man?" McCall frankly replied, "I didn't want to commit suicide."

Wild and woolly Deadwood was scourged by a devastating fire in 1879 and by a roaring flood four years later. But the enormous Homestake Mine (the largest gold mine in the Western Hemisphere), along with other mines, continued rich production, and Deadwood was rebuilt again and again.

The town remained lively for years. In 1897, for example, Wild Bunch outlaw Harvey Logan and two accomplices escaped from the Deadwood jail, and on June 12 of that year, the last legal hanging in South Dakota took the life of Isadore Cavanaugh, convicted of murdering a woman with a meat cleaver.

Today, tourists can visit Deadwood's historic sites—including the graves of Wild Bill Hickok and Calamity Jane—or they may indulge their sporting instincts at one of the town's gambling establishments.

During its heyday, Deadwood's Main Street was routinely jammed with "bull trains" and tall freight wagons; teamsters could barely keep up with the demand for supplies.

Deadwood boomed with the discovery of gold, but open-pit copper mining added even more wealth to the area economy.

Top photo: A gas-powered trolley car transports tourists around Deadwood's historic downtown district.
Bottom photo: Despite the obvious 20th-century trappings, Main Street retains much of its Old West flavor.

Top photo: Deadwood has long depended on tourism, which was greatly stimulated with the recent introduction of casino gambling. **Bottom photo:** One of many casinos in downtown Deadwood.

PRINCE OF PISTOLEERS
WILD BILL HICKOCK

Wild Bill Hickok was famous as the "Prince of Pistoleers" when he arrived in Deadwood in the spring of 1876. Hickok had killed at least seven men in seven gunfights; he had served the Federal Army as a scout during the Civil War and during Indian campaigns; he had worn a badge in rowdy Abilene and Hays City; and he had been a Wild West Show performer.

On March 5, 1876, he ended his bachelorhood three weeks before his 39th birthday, marrying 50-year-old Agnes Lake in Cheyenne, Wyoming. Agnes was a circus owner and an old acquaintance, but two weeks after their marriage, Wild Bill left his bride to seek excitement in the West's latest boomtown.

He wrote to Agnes that he was hard at work as a prospector, but all of his gold-seeking was done at a poker table in Deadwood's Number 10 Saloon. During the afternoon of August 2, Hickok entered a game with three friends, but was cleaned out within half an hour; he borrowed $50 from the house to stay in the game. A little after four o'clock, Wild Bill was dealt a queen, a pair of aces, and a pair of eights— a combination about to become famous as the "Dead Man's Hand."

A young drifter named Jack McCall suddenly walked up behind Hickok and triggered a .45-calibre slug into the back of his head, killing him instantly. Although Hickok died in debt, and a raffle of his possessions was necessary to pay his funeral expenses, his grave at Mount Moriah Cemetery became Deadwood's premier tourist attraction.

Site of Number 10 Saloon, where Wild Bill Hickok was murdered by Jack McCall on August 2, 1876. The original watering hole was consumed in the fire of 1879.

It seems inevitable that one of the West's most colorful characters would turn up in one of the West's most colorful communities.

Calamity Jane, born Martha Jane Cannary, was a tough, hard-drinking woman with a taste for the wild side of frontier life. Orphaned at an early age, she spent many of her early adult years wandering around the West, working as a cook, a dance-hall girl, and at other jobs.

Arriving in Deadwood in 1876, she became a bullwhacker, hauling machinery and supplies to area mining camps. It was here that she befriended Wild Bill Hickok and eventually captured the attention of several magazine writers whose stories—some true, some not—turned her into a Western legend.

She married Charley Burke, a hack driver, in 1891, and in 1895 began touring the Midwest with several different Wild West Shows. Her longtime fondness for alcohol eventually took its toll, however, and when she was fired from the Pan-American Exposition in 1901, she returned to Deadwood and faded from public view.

Calamity Jane died on August 1, 1903, but arranged to have August 2—Hickok's death date—placed on her marker and to be buried next to him. Perhaps it was a gesture of affection, but it suggested a closeness between them that apparently had not existed in real life.

Opposite page: Deadwood's Mt. Moriah Cemetery contains the grave sites of two famous Western characters, Wild Bill Hickok and Calamity Jane. **Left:** Occasionally mistaken for a man, Calamity Jane liked to wear men's clothing and was equally comfortable handling a rifle.

MEDORA
NORTH DAKOTA

Medora, in western North Dakota, was founded by a dreamer, but like many other frontier communities built on hope and ambition, the town faced rapid decline when these hopes and ambitions could not be realized.

The aspiring entrepreneur who created Medora was an unlikely Westerner: Antoine Amedee Marie Vincent Amat Manca de Vallombrosa, otherwise known as the Marquis de Mores.

Born in France in 1858 and trained to be a cavalry officer, the Marquis was both intelligent and energetic. Bored by army routine in peacetime, he resigned his commission and, on a trip to Paris, met Medora von Hoffman, daughter of a wealthy New York banker who had taken his family to France for a vacation. The Marquis courted Medora and married her in 1882.

The family returned to New York, where the Marquis accepted a

In 1883, the Marquis de Mores named the town for his wife and began erecting buildings; within a year there were three hotels and a dozen stores. Today, some of the old structures are still in use.

The 26-room Chateau Mores sits on a hill overlooking Medora. **Inset photo:** Oil painting of Medora von Hoffman.

position in his father-in-law's bank. But a cousin excited the Marquis with tales of a hunting trip to the Dakota Badlands, and the budding frontier visionary managed to interest his bride's father in an investment centered around the era's fabled Beef Bonanza.

The Marquis discovered an ideal townsite where the Northern Pacific Railroad crossed the Little Missouri River, and in April of 1883, he smashed a bottle of wine over a tent and christened the headquarters of his dream empire Medora, in honor of his vivacious and headstrong wife.

The Marquis established the Northern Pacific Refrigerator Car Company and built an immense slaughterhouse on the outskirts of Medora, intending to process cattle from area ranches—including his own—and ship meat to the East by refrigerator car. Operations began within a few months, and the Marquis organized a chain of icehouses and cold-storage plants along the Northern Pacific route.

On a bluff across the river from Medora, the Marquis built "The Chateau," a rambling, two-story ranch house with 26 rooms and luxurious appointments. In town, he constructed a two-story brick office building, a brick church for his wife, and a large brick house to accommodate his in-laws when they visited (the latter two structures and the ranch house still stand).

On the business front, the Marquis opened a freight route to Deadwood, 200 miles to the south, as well as a stagecoach line, and he founded a company to ship salmon from the Pacific Northwest to New York City.

This infusion of capital stimulated other construction, and by the end of 1884, a population of 250 enjoyed three hotels and a dozen stores. The Marquis and Marquise, who was as good a shot as her husband, staged elaborate hunting expeditions, traveled to Yellowstone National Park, and entertained her parents, rancher Theodore Roosevelt, and other interesting guests. They were the town's leading citizens, but many Westerners were offended by the air of nobility exuded by the Marquis: When challenged by a trio of drunken ruffians, he shot one to death, then won acquittal during a trial that elicited enormous local interest.

Despite his skills as a cavalryman, the Marquis was not an experienced businessman, and his overly ambitious schemes ultimately proved unsound, costing him and his father-in-law well over a million dollars. By 1886, all of his ventures had failed. He returned to France the next year, became embroiled in various political controversies, fought several duels, and was murdered in North Africa in 1896.

The Marquise raised her three children in France, but returned occasionally to Medora. Eventually, the de Mores family donated the Chateau and other property in the village to the State of North Dakota, and today Medora is a popular tourist site.

Above: The Marquis (standing, just right of center) in 1884 with a hunting party at the rear of the Chateau de Mores. A former French cavalry officer, the Marquis was a superb horseman and a crack shot. **Right:** The Marquis with his beloved Medora, who often galloped to the hunt with him.

Opposite page, top: Overview of Medora in 1908. In the lower right foreground is the house (with two chimneys) that the Marquis built for his in-laws, the von Hoffmans, for their summer visits to Medora. Just beyond is the Catholic church built in 1884. The meatpacking plant built by the Marquis burned in 1907, but the tall brick chimney is visible in the background. **Opposite page, bottom:** The Medora Stage and Forwarding Company operated between Medora and Deadwood in 1884 and 1885. **Left:** Medora's citizens have spared their legendary hanging tree, even though it sits in the middle of a street. **Below:** The Rough Riders Hotel, where Theodore Roosevelt made speeches from the balcony at right.

WESTERN RANCHER
TEDDY ROOSEVELT

"If it had not been for my years in North Dakota," declared Theodore Roosevelt, "I never would have become President of the United States."

It was the desire to shoot a buffalo "while there were still buffalo to shoot" that initially brought the native New Yorker to the Dakota Badlands. Here, the 24-year-old future president met the flamboyant Marquis de Mores, reveled in the rugged vastness of the terrain, finally bagged his buffalo, and purchased the Maltese Cross Ranch, eight miles south of Medora.

The next year, Roosevelt's mother and his lovely wife, who had just given birth, died on the same day. Hungering for solitude, a grieving Roosevelt returned to the Maltese Cross in June of 1884, then acquired a second

Theodore Roosevelt, rancher and hunter, in 1884.

spread in a lonely wilderness 30 miles north of Medora.

On his new Elkhorn Ranch, Roosevelt built an eight-room log cabin where, between hunting expeditions, he mastered the cowboy's skills. Since childhood Roosevelt had been plagued with health problems and a spindly physique, but rigorous exercise in the clear air of the West was the turning point in his battle for health. His body developed powerfully, and his despair faded as he zestfully threw himself into the primitive lifestyle of a frontier rancher.

A prolific author, Roosevelt wrote compulsively at his Elkhorn cabin, penning several books on Western subjects and many articles about his frontier experiences. But in 1886 and 1887, disastrous range conditions cost Roosevelt most of his $85,000 investment.

Soon, Roosevelt returned to New York, where he remarried and resumed his political career as a member of the Civil Service Commission. He continued to be influenced by the West, however, returning there regularly to hunt.

Top photo: Porch of the sprawling cabin of Theodore Roosevelt's Elkhorn Ranch, located 30 miles north of Medora. Seated on this porch, Roosevelt wrote articles and books about his Western experiences.

Bottom photo: Roosevelt's first Dakota ranch was the Maltese Cross, eight miles south of Medora. The cabin has been moved to Medora, where it may be toured at the entrance to Theodore Roosevelt National Park.

CALDWELL
KANSAS

aldwell was a trail town of such unrestrained violence that it proved fatal for more law officers than any other Kansas community.

In 1880, George Flatt, at one time an effective city marshal, was killed in an ambush as he lurched drunkenly down Main Street during a midnight spree. A few months later, assistant marshal Frank Hunt was shot to death in Caldwell's infamous Red Light Saloon. In 1881, mayor and former marshal Mike Meagher was killed during a street fight. The following year, city marshal George Brown was gunned down when he tried to arrest a pair of trouble-making Texans.

What manner of town was this to sport such a casualty rate among its chief representatives of law and order? Dubbed the "Border Queen" because its southern limits coincided with the line between Kansas and Oklahoma, Caldwell also benefited from its position astride the fabled Chisholm Trail. By the

Mural of Caldwell, the "Border Queen," painted on a Main Street building.

Caldwell seems so peaceful today that it's hard to imagine it as the wild frontier town it once was.

early 1870s, a few ramshackle saloons and stores had been built on either side of Chisholm Street, catering to the lusty tastes and needs of the drovers who annually herded hundreds of thousands of cattle north to the railheads—first to Abilene, then Ellsworth, Newton, and finally Wichita, 50 miles north of Caldwell.

When farmers secured legislation to bar Texas cattle from Kansas, it was reasoned that if the railroad were extended from Wichita down to Caldwell, stockyards built south of town (with a gate in Oklahoma) could handle longhorns without violating the technicalities of the law. In 1880, the Atchison, Topeka & Santa Fe stretched its tracks into Caldwell, which then became the terminus of the West's most famous cattle trail.

A boom promptly ensued, and the center of town shifted uphill and a block to the west.

Looking north on Caldwell's Main Street in 1889, as homesteaders drive through town in their covered wagons, gathering provisions before the first big Oklahoma land rush.

The flimsy buildings of Chisholm Street were forsaken for more substantial masonry structures, many of which still stand today on Main Street.

A dozen saloons flourished, but the most popular commercial establishment was A. S. Groh's Cheap Cash Chicago Store, which catered to Texas cowboys. So did the Lone Star Clothing House and many other local businesses. There were livery stables, restaurants, lumberyards, jewelry stores, two newspapers, three churches, several barber shops, a bookshop, and a Chinese laundry. A city well was dug at the primary intersection of Main Street, and a two-story brick school was erected west of the business section in 1881-82.

By this time, boom conditions had triggered a clash between cattlemen and merchants, who soon became known respectively as "south-enders" and "north-enders." In 1881, stockmen built a vast brick Opera House that dominated the south end of town until it burned in 1918. The merchants enviously planned their own civic auditorium, to be located at the north end of the business district, but financial reality persuaded them to desist.

Community leaders next recognized the inadequacies of Caldwell's hostelries. South-enders began to organize a group of financial backers for a substantial hotel, and north-enders immediately countered with a hotel firm of their own.

Two three-story brick edifices soon were erected on different corners of the west side of Main Street. The Leland Hotel boasted 50 rooms, a view of Indian Territory, and the finest dining facilities in Caldwell. A windmill behind the hotel provided water for patrons. At the north end of town was the Southwestern Hotel, featuring a second-floor ladies' parlor and 38 rooms. When a new city hall and jail were constructed, they were diplomatically situated in the center of the business district just off Main Street.

The town's leadership decided that it could not tolerate the unbridled violence that had plagued Caldwell in the form of gunfights since 1871. Indeed, Eastern cattle buyers might avoid a town where they felt in danger. Accordingly, in 1882 the city marshal's badge was pinned on Henry Brown, a two-gun terror who had ridden with Billy the Kid and who quickly tamed Caldwell by killing the worst of the troublemakers in two separate shootouts.

In 1881, an impressive brick Opera House was officially opened with a traveling troupe's performance of *Uncle Tom's Cabin.* The imposing structure dominated the south end of town until it burned in 1918.

Penetration of Texas by railroads virtually closed the Chisholm Trail by 1885, and Caldwell began to settle into a subdued existence. Frontier exuberance was revived for a time in 1893, when the Cherokee Strip was opened to settlers. The six-million-acre tract was located just below Caldwell, and the town suddenly teemed with homesteaders. At noon on September 16, 1893, Caldwell witnessed the West's final tumultuous land rush.

Today the land rush is only a memory, as are the cowboys and gunfighters who were once part of the landscape. Bypassed by Interstate 35, some 15 miles to the east, Caldwell today is surrounded by wheat farms. But while other Kansas cattle towns grew and changed, Caldwell has kept much of its frontier flavor.

Above: A sign at the corner of Fifth and Main pinpoints the location where the Southwestern Hotel once stood at the north end of Caldwell's business district. **Right:** Shown here in an 1886 photo, the hotel boasted 38 rooms and a second-floor ladies' parlor. Gunfighter Henry Brown lived in the hotel while he served as Caldwell's city marshal.

Top photo: Caldwell in 1888. The large brick building to the right of center is the Opera House, while the new, two-story school is visible in the background at left. **Above:** Customers and employees pose for a photo at the Stock Exchange Bank in 1881.

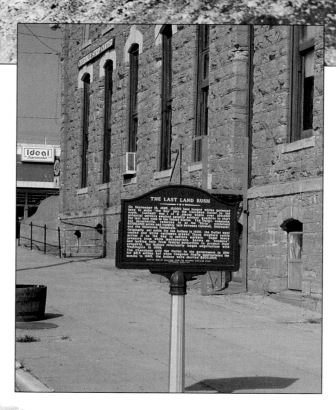

Above: Huge crowds of people awaited the opening of Oklahoma's Cherokee Strip on September 16, 1893. More than 100,000 potential settlers gathered at nine approved locations to surge into the six-million-acre Strip. As one of the designated staging areas, Caldwell teemed with an estimated 15,000 home-steaders. **Right:** A historical marker on a Caldwell side street commemorates "The Last Land Rush." The building in the background was a bank, but today houses an excellent museum.

Above: Looking north on Caldwell's busy Main Street. Prominent on the corner of Main and Sixth was the three-story Leland Hotel. A windmill behind the 50-room Leland provided water for the patrons, and Oklahoma could be seen from the third-floor windows. Caldwell's other three-story hotel, the South-western, is visible on the same side of the street at the north end of the business district. In the middle of the block was the Lone Star Clothing House, which catered to Texas cowboys. **Left:** Historical marker in a Main Street park describes the town's violent past, when, as an early editor remarked, "hell was in session in Caldwell." The marker concludes: "Caldwell of the past was home to gunslingers, cowboys, prostitutes, Indians, saloon keepers, and criminals; but around this sign today is a proud, quiet, farming community made up of good citizens instilling its small-town values in its youth...."

CALDWELL "THE BORDER QUEEN"

Founded 1871, incorporated 1879 by a town company of investors from Wichita and named for U. S. Sen. Alexander Caldwell. The original townsite laid north of Ave. F, the Kansas state line prior to 1876. One of the original cowtowns in Kansas, violence and politics claimed 16 city marshals between 1879 and 1885 and led a Wichita editor to write "As we go to press hell is again in session in Caldwell". Founded on the Chisholm Trail, which was 200 - 400 yards wide and ran just east of this park in a northerly direction. Caldwell acted as a railroad shipping point for Texas longhorn cattle. By 1886 the cattle shipping had moved west as farmers settled the area and planted their Russian hard winter wheat. In 1893 congress opened to settlement the Cherokee outlet, and thousands of land hungry pioneers staged here before making the last great land rush in America. Caldwell of the past was home to gunslingers, cowboys, prostitutes, Indians, saloon keepers, and criminals; but around this sign today is a proud, quiet, farming community made up of good citizens instilling its small - town values in its youth... though, as Bill O'Neal wrote of Caldwell in 1980. "In just the right light it is not difficult to imagine the sounds of a frontier saloon, of cattle hooves, and gunfire".

(Continued on other side)

ERECTED 1993 BY BORDER QUEEN MUSEUM BOARD AND ROSE ELLEN WOOD
IN MEMORY OF DR. L. CURTICE WOOD, PH.D. 1911-1991

Right: Caldwell's *Weekly Advance* press room in the early 1900s. Twenty years earlier, Caldwell boasted three newspapers: the *Commercial,* the *Journal,* and the *Post.* **Below:** Group photo of Caldwell's volunteer firemen in the 1890s.

THE WARPATH OF HENRY BROWN

Born in Missouri in 1857, Henry Newton Brown headed west at the age of 17, learning the cowboy's trade and spending a season hunting buffalo. In 1876, a quarrel in a Texas Panhandle cattle camp led to gunplay, and Henry pumped three slugs into his unlucky adversary.

Subsequently, he gravitated to turbulent New Mexico, where he became a participant in the bloody Lincoln County War. Brown was indicted for murder (unsuccessfully), and he fought in numerous shootouts, including the climactic five-day battle in Lincoln. Afterward, he teamed up with Billy the Kid and various other fugitives, who formed a band of horse and cattle thieves.

In 1878, Billy the Kid, Brown, and three other rustlers moved a herd of stolen horses to the Tascosa area of the Texas

Bank robbers John Wesley, Henry Brown (wearing the light-colored hat and bandanna), William Smith, and Ben Wheeler are assembled in front of the Medicine Lodge jail shortly after their capture. All four men would be dead by morning, victims of vigilante justice.

Panhandle. Brown stayed, working as a stock detective and as a cowboy, although he was fired because, as he once put it, he was "always on the warpath." Next, Brown pinned on a deputy sheriff's badge, but was discharged again because he was found to be too violent. By 1882, he had become city marshal of lawless Caldwell, which welcomed the kind of service that Brown was willing to provide. The aggressive gunfighter quickly tamed the Border Queen, and grateful citizens presented the marshal with a magnificent engraved Winchester, raising his pay to $125 per month.

But just one month after marrying a local lass, Marshal Brown returned to his wicked ways, leading his deputy and two other gunmen in robbing a bank 70 miles to the west in Medicine Lodge. The bank president and a cashier were killed, but the outlaw marshal and his gang were captured. Brown was shot that night, trying to escape. The others were lynched.

After the Chisholm Trail closed in 1886, the raucous Border Queen became a quiet farming town. The Southwestern Hotel stood just beyond the last two-story brick building in the center of the photo.

Top photo: Today, Caldwell is surrounded by wheat farms. Interestingly, the population remains about the same (1,600) as it was during the cowtown's heyday. **Bottom photo:** No longer in service, this old Union Pacific caboose now serves as a plaything for Caldwell's youngsters. When the first railroad reached Caldwell in 1880, the Border Queen became the terminus of the Chisholm Trail.

INGALLS
OKLAHOMA

On September 1, 1893, one of the West's most spectacular battles between outlaws and lawmen was fought in the streets of Ingalls, Oklahoma. The town had become a resort for Bill Doolin's gang of "Oklahombres," and the unfavorable attention attracted by the bloody shootout doomed Ingalls to eventual ghost status.

Oklahoma's first land rush occurred on April 22, 1889, onto Unassigned Lands released to settlers in large part through the efforts of Kansas Senator John James Ingalls. Six counties were organized, and most of the 160-acre tracts were quickly claimed by homesteaders.

This rural population needed nearby communities for provisions and mail, and small towns sprang up throughout the region. In eastern Payne County, two progressive settlers, Dr. Robert F. McMurtry and Robert Beal, each donated 40 acres for a townsite to be named after Senator Ingalls.

At the north end of Ash Street, Ingalls's main thoroughfare, a monument to fallen lawmen and an old cabin serve as reminders of the town's early history.

Not much is left of Ingalls. Less than two dozen people live in the community today.

Ingalls was surrounded by fertile prairie lands. The Cimarron River was just to the southeast, and other streams also were nearby. McMurtry and Beal had their 80 acres surveyed into a square townsite of 16 blocks, with 100-foot-wide streets and 20-foot-wide alleys. The four east-west streets were numbered from the north: First, Second, Third, and Fourth. The four north-south streets, beginning from the west, were Main, Walnut, Ash, and Oak.

Beal opened a general store and corral, while Dr. McMurtry built a frame structure for a drugstore and undertaking parlor. McMurtry was elected town coroner, and on January 22, 1890,

he was appointed postmaster. But the doctor was stricken with health problems, and he relinquished the position of postmaster to J. W. Ellsworth, a part-time minister and notary public. When McMurtry died, his widow turned the frame building into a notions shop.

Dr. W. R. Call opened a pharmacy, and within the next few years three other physicians—J. L. Briggs, D. H. Selph, and Jacob Pickering—arrived with their families. Two blacksmith shops went up, along with a barber shop, a dry goods store, a hardware store, a boot shop, and a gristmill. Before long, other general stores, livery stables, and several saloons were built. The sole two-story

Measuring 100 feet across, Ash Street was still a busy thoroughfare in 1899, and outbursts of violence were not uncommon.

structure in town was the O.K. Hotel. A number of houses were constructed, and, of course, there were nearby homesteads. In 1891, the town's school boasted 40 students. A city well was installed at Ash and Second, the town's main intersection.

A brothel was located near the O. K. Hotel, and beer and whiskey flowed plentifully in the saloons. Fistfights were common, and there was a fatal shooting in 1892 and another the following year. By that time Bill Doolin and his outlaw friends were in the habit of slipping into town, drinking and gambling and patronizing the brothel. In addition to these recreational pursuits, the outlaws visited the barber shop, sought treatment for illnesses and wounds from the town's doctors, traded horses and had their mounts shod, and purchased provisions from the stores.

Students and teachers in front of the Ingalls school around the turn of the century. **Inset photo:** Surviving today as the oldest school building in Payne County, the structure has been moved just north of the old townsite, where it serves as a civic center and museum.

When the gang visited Ingalls on September 1, 1893, Doolin, Bill Dalton, Bitter Creek Newcomb, Tulsa Jack Blake, Red Buck Waightman, and Dynamite Dick Clifton bellied up to the bar of the Ransom and Murray Saloon, while an ailing Arkansas Tom Jones went to an upstairs room of the O.K. Hotel to collapse into bed.

A short time later, 13 deputy U. S. marshals quietly moved into town in three covered wagons, and when Bitter Creek Newcomb stepped out-side for some air, lawman Dick Speed took a shot at him. Newcomb's cohorts assembled quickly to back him up, and in an instant the lead was flying.

The most damaging shots of the furious ex-change were fired by Arkansas Jones from his up-stairs vantage point. Deputies Speed, Tom Hueston, and Lafe Shadley were fatally wounded, as were two townspeople. Two other civilians were hit, along with Newcomb, but Bitter Creek

Above left: The only two-story building in Ingalls was the O.K. Hotel. Arkansas Tom Jones, sleeping upstairs when fighting erupted, shot lawman Dick Speed from the rear window, poked a hole in the west roof to drill deputy Tom Hueston, then shot Lafe Shadley from a front window. **Above right:** Monument to the three fallen officers.

and the other outlaws managed to gallop out of town, abandoning Jones to capture.

After the Battle of Ingalls, attempts by the city fathers to regain respectability were dashed by continued gunfights. Lurid tales prompted travelers to avoid Ingalls, and when railroads missed the town, one of the toughest frontier communities of the 1890s began its permanent decline.

Below: The Ransom and Murray Saloon, which faced east on Ash Street. During the Battle of Ingalls, outlaws Bill Doolin, Bill Dalton, Dynamite Dick Clifton, and Tulsa Jack Blake dashed out of the building to escape under fire. **Right:** Today, the headquarters of Caldwell's Volunteer Fire Department is located near the site where lawman Dick Speed fell.

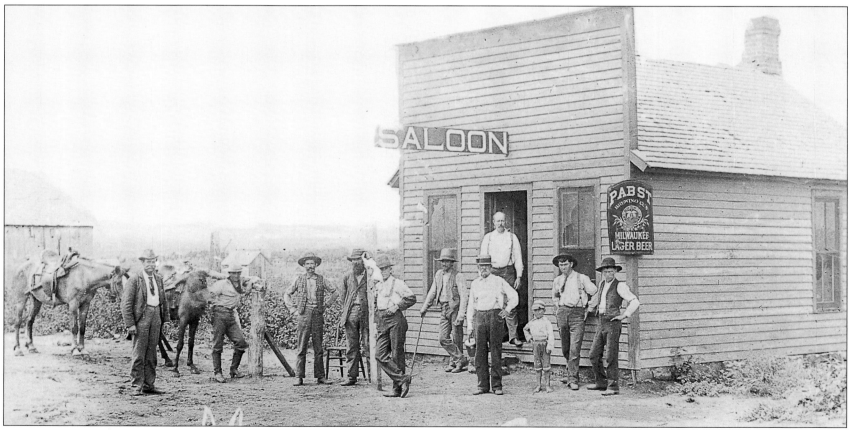

OKLAHOMA OUTLAW
BILL DOOLIN

The leader of the Oklahombres was born in 1858 and reared on his family's Arkansas farm. Doolin drifted into Indian Territory in 1881 and began working as a cowboy. By 1891, he had become a ranch foreman.

That same year, Doolin and a group of cowboys threw a Fourth of July beer bust just outside Coffeyville, Kansas. When two constables tried to break up the party, a fight broke out and both officers were killed. Afraid he would be blamed, Doolin fled and soon joined the infamous Dalton gang.

Doolin participated in numerous train and bank holdups, though he was not present in 1892 when the Dalton gang was destroyed while attempting to rob two Coffeyville banks simultaneously.

Doolin married a preacher's daughter from Ingalls but, unreformed, eventually organized his own gang. From 1893 through 1895, the Oklahombres specialized in robbing banks. Doolin was arrested by peace officer Bill Tilghman early in 1896, but the outlaw leader escaped jail and hid out on the New Mexico ranch of writer Eugene Manlove Rhodes.

Doolin rejoined his wife and son at Lawson, Oklahoma, but on the night of August 25, 1896, he was gunned down by a posse led by lawman Heck Thomas. Within a short time, all of Doolin's Oklahombres were either killed or captured.

Above: Bill Tilghman, famed peace officer who captured Bill Doolin in a health resort at Eureka Springs, Arkansas, although the outlaw later escaped jail. In 1924, Tilghman was shot to death while still wearing a badge at the age of 70. **Right:** Lawman Heck Thomas, one of Oklahoma's "Three Guardsmen" (along with Bill Tilghman and Chris Madsen). A fearless and deadly officer, Thomas led the posse that cornered Doolin at the home of his father-in-law. When Doolin tried to fight, Thomas and a deputy shot him dead.

Cowboys from the Texas-Oklahoma Panhandle photographed at mealtime in 1885. Outlaw Bill Doolin and several members of his gang had worked as cowboys in the same region before turning to crime for their livelihoods.

Top photo: Old low-water crossing on the Cimarron River, five miles south of Ingalls. **Right:** The land formation known as East Round Mountain, facing east. **Opposite page:** Marker for the Battle of Round Mountains. Oklahoma's first Civil War battle occurred three decades before nearby Ingalls was born. The so-called Five Civilized Tribes of Indian Territory were from the South, and many from their ranks owned slaves. An Indian brigade fought for the Confederacy, and Cherokee Stand Watie became a Confederate brigadier general.

TASCOSA
TEXAS

Tascosa sprang up beside the Canadian River in the Texas Panhandle in the mid-1870s, just as the buffalo herds and the Comanches and Kiowas were disappearing from the landscape. Great cattle ranches such as the LS, the LIT, the Frying Pan, and the three-million-acre XIT developed in the vicinity, and for nearly two decades Tascosa proudly proclaimed itself the "Cowboy Capital of the Panhandle."

Tascosa's frame school was built at the north end of town. Later renovated as a private residence, it is one of only two buildings that remain from the era when Tascosa was known as the "Cowboy Capital of the Panhandle."

Indeed, the West's only cowboy strike occurred in Tascosa in 1883, this while herds in the region were owned by such legendary cattle barons as Charles Goodnight, John Chisum, and George Littlefield.

Tascosa's Boot Hill included victims from one of the deadliest saloon fights in frontier history. Billy the Kid, Pat Garrett, Henry Brown, and Temple Houston were among the lethal gunfighters who rode the town's dusty streets, and when the cowboys, gunmen, gam-

The only two-story building in Tascosa was the stone courthouse, built in 1884. After the dying town lost its position as the seat of Oldham County, the abandoned courthouse was purchased by Julian Bivins, who added a porch to what became his ranch headquarters (visible in background).

Above left: The great pioneer cattleman Charles Goodnight, a former Texas Ranger who blazed cattle trails, invented the chuck wagon, and founded a number of ranches, the most famous of which was the JA in Palo Duro Canyon. **Above right:** Cattle baron John Chisum was from Texas, but his enormous ranching enterprise was in eastern New Mexico, where 100,000 cattle ranged up and down the Pecos River.

blers, bartenders, and "soiled doves" finally abandoned the site a few years before the turn of the century, Tascosa played the final role of the classic Western community, crumbling picturesquely into an adobe-piled ghost town.

A creek known as Atascosa (an Indian word for "boggy," because wagons would bog down in the quicksand) flowed into the Canadian River at a good crossing, and it was there in 1876 that blacksmith Henry Kimball erected a one-room adobe—the first Anglo-American structure in the upper Panhandle. Soon, two merchants from New Mexico built an adobe general store, initially stocked with three barrels of whiskey and a few boxes of soda crackers, but later boasting far more varied merchandise.

Assorted businesses dedicated to serving the ranches and its cowboys were established along a two-block Main Street that ran east and west. The Exchange Hotel was the town's only hostelry, the *Tascosa Pioneer* became the only newspaper, and the Equity Bar was Tascosa's first—and most famous—saloon. A cluster of dives a quarter of a mile east of Main Street was dubbed Hogtown, partially because of the presence of such less than glamorous "sporting women" as Homely Ann, Gizzard Lip, Rowdy Kate, Box Car Jane, Panhandle Nan, Slippery Sue, Canadian Lily, and Frog Lip Sadie.

In 1878, Billy the Kid and four other fugitives from New Mexico's Lincoln County War arrived with 150 stolen horses, enjoying Tascosa's bawdy pleasures for several weeks. During the 1880s, there was so much rustling that Pat Garrett was hired to lead a band of "Home Rangers." The first of Tascosa's 10 gunfights erupted in 1881, its casualties buried in Boot Hill just west of town.

When businessmen applied for a post office at "Atascosa," they were informed that another Texas community already had claimed the name. So the "A" was dropped from the spelling, as it already had been in pronunciation, and Tascosa became the seat of newly organized Oldham County. The population reached 600, with additional numbers of cowboys and ranchers who regularly rode in from the surrounding countryside to patronize the stores and saloons.

But a long drought hurt area ranches, then broke disastrously in 1893 with heavy rains that flooded the Canadian. The river's wagon bridge was swept away, along with the footbridge across Tascosa Creek, and 17 buildings were destroyed when their flat roofs caved in. Soon, merely a

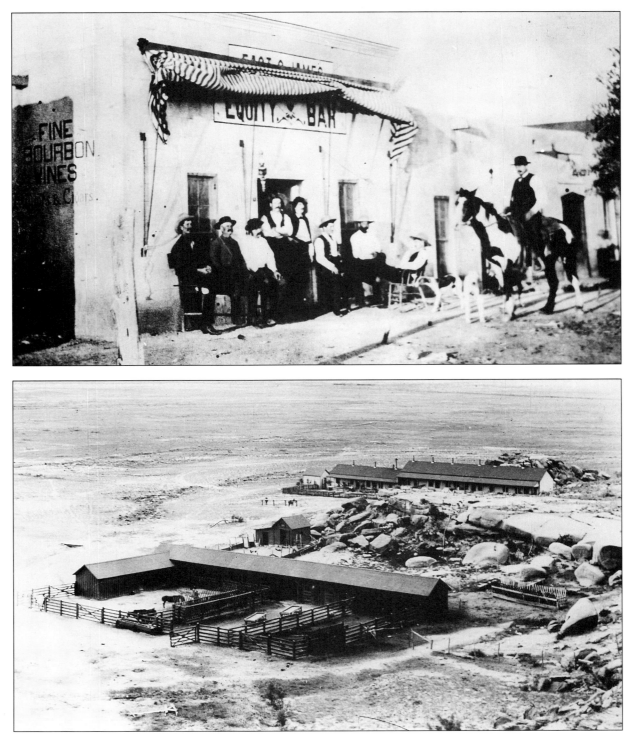

Top photo: Tascosa's most famous saloon, the Equity Bar, stood on the north side of Main Street. In 1881, Sheriff Cape Willingham rounded the corner at left and blasted troublemaker Fred Leigh out of the saddle with a shotgun. Mounted man in picture (thought to be Willingham) is about where Leigh died.

Bottom photo: LS Ranch headquarters, located about four miles southeast of Tascosa. During its peak years, 150 LS cowboys herded 50,000 cattle over a rangeland nearly the size of Connecticut. The buildings at left, which formed the third LS headquarters, were erected in 1893 and today are at the center of what remains of the historic ranch.

handful of the remaining structures were occupied, and Tascosa slumped into permanent decline. In 1915, the new town of Vega wrested away the county seat.

Tascosa's adobe buildings lost their plaster and roofs, then slowly crumbled. Julian Bivins purchased the old stone courthouse, added a front porch, and converted the two-story structure into a ranch headquarters. Frenchy McCormick, who had come to Tascosa as a bride in 1880, stayed on among the ruins as the last Tascosan until 1939, when she moved to be with friends. When she died two years later, she was interred at Boot Hill beside her husband.

But 1939 marked an unexpected rebirth for the one-time cattle town. Philanthropist Cal Farley organized a Boys Ranch for unfortunate youths, and from a modest beginning, the institution now boasts a complex of modern buildings atop the former town site, as well as a population that rivals Tascosa in its frontier heyday.

All that remains from the 19th century are the courthouse, now a museum; the frame school, converted into an attractive residence; and Boot Hill, last home of the pioneers who lived, fought, and died in the Cowboy Capital of the Panhandle.

Inset photo: Young Frenchy McCormick came to Tascosa in 1880 as the bride of Mickey McCormick, who ran the town's livery stable. **Above right:** Widowed in 1912, Frenchy stubbornly maintained her crumbling adobe home west of Tascosa Creek, eventually becoming the town's last resident. In 1939, Frenchy moved to a friend's home in Channing, to the north, where she died two years later.

In 1939, philanthropist Cal Farley purchased Tascosa's 1884 courthouse and organized a Boys Ranch for unfortunate youths. From a modest beginning, the institution now boasts a complex of modern buildings atop the former townsite. At upper right is the old courthouse, now a museum. **Inset photo:** The inscription beneath the statue of Cal Farley with one of his young charges reads: "It's Where You Are Going That Counts."

THE SHORT-LIVED COWBOY STRIKE

Feeling little loyalty to absentee owners and cattle syndicates who kept cowboy wages at $25 per month, drovers signed an agreement demanding $50 per month for cowboys and cooks and $75 monthly for foremen. A strike date was set for April 1, 1883. Leader of the movement was Tom Lee—who was already being paid $100 monthly as foreman of the LS Ranch. Lee was fired, and so were the other cowboys when they presented their demands. The T-Anchor Ranch headquarters were fortified, and when a committee of strikers approached, they were abruptly scattered by rifle bullets.

Nearly 100 striking cowpunchers gathered in Tascosa, but after a few days in Hogtown their money vanished. Area ranchers had no trouble finding replacements, and within a few weeks the strike collapsed. Most of the unsuccessful strikers drifted out of the county, but a few hung on, establishing their own little spreads. To supplement their "retirements," some former cowboys felt justified in occasionally snatching the unbranded calves of the big outfits.

Below: Cowboys from the LIT Ranch. Almost 100 drovers from ranches around Tascosa took part in the cowboy strike of 1883.

XIT Ranch cowboys. The enormous ranch extended from the northwest corner of the Texas Panhandle more than 200 miles down the Texas-New Mexico border. It took 6,000 miles of barbed wire to fence the 10 divisions of the 3,050,000-acre ranch. This vast acreage was deeded to a Chicago syndicate, which in return agreed to build a massive new state capitol.

Branding irons and saddles are among the historical artifacts on display at the Julian Bivins Museum, located in Tascosa's old courthouse at Cal Farley's Boys Ranch. Also on display is a scale model of Tascosa during the 1880s.

TASCOSA'S
BIG FIGHT

At two o'clock, on the morning of March 21, 1886, Tascosa's bloodiest shootout erupted at the town's main intersection. LS Ranch cowboys Ed King, Fred Chilton, Frank Valley, and John Lang left a dance in Hogtown to seek further recreation in Tascosa. As they passed the Jenkins and Dunn Saloon, King, who had been joined by "sporting lady" Sally Emory, exchanged insults with several men on the porch.

As King strolled off, arm in arm with Sally, a gunshot from the porch dropped him in his tracks. Lem Woodruff, a cowboy who had been trying to win Sally's affections, ran into the street and fired a Winchester slug into the fallen King's throat.

"Boys, they've killed Ed," shouted John Lang. "Come on!"

Brandishing their revolvers, Lang, Chilton, and Valley slipped into the rear of the saloon, and a barrage of gunfire exploded inside. Woodruff caught two bullets low in the abdomen, while his friend, Charley Emory, was hit in the leg. As Woodruff staggered away, Valley gave chase, but was felled by a slug in the left eye.

Jesse Sheets, owner of the North Star Restaurant next door, unwisely appeared in the saloon doorway in his nightclothes. Chilton killed him with a bullet to the forehead, but his gun flash brought two rounds tearing into his chest. Chilton handed his six-gun to Lang and died. Lang retreated outside, exchanging furious fire with the men in the saloon, just as two lawmen sprinted onto the scene, ending what came to be known as "The Big Fight."

Above left: Tascosa's Jenkins and Dunn Saloon, site of the 1886 shootout in which four men were killed. **Above right:** Across the street from the saloon was Wright and Farnsworth's General Store, where the bodies of Ed King, Fred Chilton, and Frank Valley were laid out on the porch and covered with a tarpaulin.

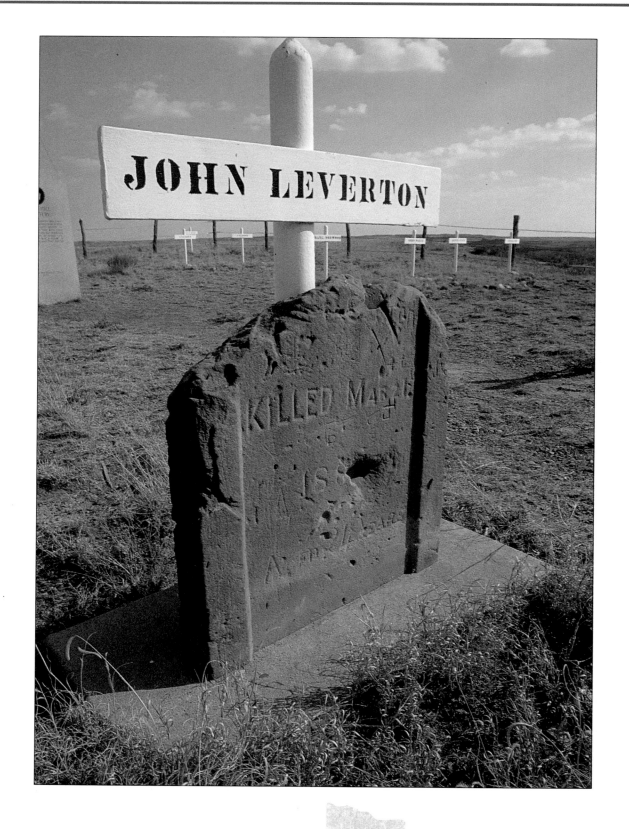

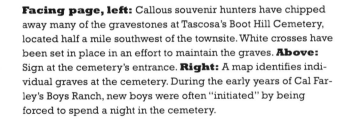

Facing page, left: Callous souvenir hunters have chipped away many of the gravestones at Tascosa's Boot Hill Cemetery, located half a mile southwest of the townsite. White crosses have been set in place in an effort to maintain the graves. **Above:** Sign at the cemetery's entrance. **Right:** A map identifies individual graves at the cemetery. During the early years of Cal Farley's Boys Ranch, new boys were often "initiated" by being forced to spend a night in the cemetery.

MOBEETIE
TEXAS

After Texas attorney Temple Houston, a two-fisted drinker and expert gunman in his own right, made his first visit to Mobeetie, he described it in a letter to his fiancée as "a baldheaded whiskey town with few virtuous women."

This wild frontier community became known as the "Mother of the Panhandle" because it was the first town in that Texas region. Buffalo hunters established a supply base on Sweetwater Creek in 1874. Their simple picket shelters, covered with buffalo hides, produced the nickname "Hidetown."

The next year the army erected its only significant Panhandle military post, Fort Elliott, just to the north. Prostitutes, gamblers, and merchants moved into Hidetown for their share of the military payroll, but when a killing occured, the army ordered all civilians off the premises.

J. T. Morrow Drugs & Sundries in downtown Mobeetie. The photo was taken in 1904, when Mobeetie was in serious decline.

No longer in use, an old barber shop and a saloon (under repair when this recent photo was taken) are among Mobeetie's oldest buildings.

Fort Elliott was established in 1875. This photograph was taken from the southeast corner of the parade grounds. Barracks are at the left, with officers' quarters behind them. Mobeetie was about a mile and a half behind the camera.

The civilian population, numbering approximately 150, moved about a mile, around a bend in the creek, and the town of Sweetwater was born. When it was discovered that the postal system already had assigned the name Sweetwater to another Texas town, "Mobeetie" (the Comanche equivalent) became the permanent label.

As Mobeetie continued to grow, a variety of businesses went up along the main street, which stretched three blocks east to west. Most of the structures were one-story frame, picket, or adobe buildings, some of which had false fronts.

"Almost every other establishment is for the purpose of dispensing liquor," noted Temple Houston. Indeed, by the 1880s Mobeetie boasted as many as 13 saloons. Houses of prostitution were located on the northwest edge of town on a slight rise called Feather Hill, so named,

according to legend, because when two women began fighting over a cowboy who wore his spurs in bed, the rowels ripped the bedding and feathers flew.

Two of the town's more memorable "soiled doves" were Frog Mouth Annie, whose constant chaw of tobacco stretched the corner of her mouth, and Diamond Girl, who always appeared in public adorned in diamonds and black satin. On one occasion when Diamond Girl was jailed, a cowboy named Jim Brady paid her fine. They took up residence together in a house north of the jail, but when she fell in love with a lieutenant from Fort Elliott, Brady killed her in a drunken rage.

The open prairie landscape was dominated by the two-story stone jail and the even more impressive two-story stone courthouse. Court sessions provided dramatic entertainment, especially when the gifted orator Temple Houston was the prosecuting attorney. Settlers and cowboys would come to Mobeetie and camp out for several days. When each day's session adjourned, there were horse races, shooting contests, and dances. These events would be climaxed by "Tournament Day," during which riders dubbed "Knights of the Lance" galloped at breakneck speed to spear as many rings as possible from a post. The winner was awarded a watch or saddle, plus the privilege of escorting the event's chosen queen to the Tournament Ball.

In 1890, with Mobeetie's population at 400, the War Department closed Fort Elliott. Panhandle railroads had already bypassed the town, and its decline was exacerbated by an 1898 tornado that killed six residents and destroyed many buildings. The county seat was moved to Wheeler in 1907, and today only the stone jail and a few frame structures remain.

J. J. Long's general store was on Mobeetie's main street, which stretched three blocks east to west. This busy street scene dates back to the 1880s, when the resident population reached 400. Bat Masterson had his first gunfight in a Mobeetie saloon on January 24, 1876; Bat was wounded, but his adversary, a corporal named King, was killed, along with saloon girl Molly Brennan.

Above: The two-story Wheeler County jail, now a museum, was built in 1889. The town's original two-story courthouse, which once stood nearby, had to be torn down years ago.
Left: Among the more unusual items found at the old jail is this makeshift gallows. **Right:** Also on display are assorted collectibles and other memorabilia from the 19th century.

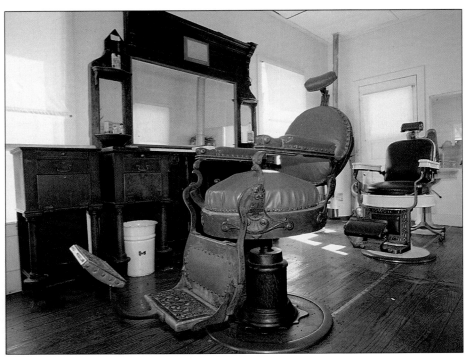

Far left: Wood-burning stove in the old jail museum. **Top center:** Interior of what may be Mobeetie's first barber shop. **Left and above:** Just south of the old townsite is the original town cemetery, founded in 1876.

THE HONEYMOON OF TEMPLE HOUSTON

Temple Houston

Temple Lea Houston was the last of eight children born to Sam and Margaret Lea Houston. In 1860, he became the first baby born in Texas's new Governors' Mansion, but his illustrious father passed away in 1863 and his mother died four years later in a yellow fever epidemic. Temple became a cowboy while in his early teens, but within a few years he entered college and was admitted to the bar at the age of 19.

"Old Sam's word-slinging son" opened a practice in Brazoria, Texas, and within a year he was elected county attorney. On his 21st birthday, he became engaged to teenaged Laura Cross, then left to assume his new duties as district attorney of the Panhandle. Temple returned to marry Laura on February 14, 1883—and thereafter he called her his "Valentine."

The young newlyweds took a train to Wichita Falls, debarking frequently for entertainment by Temple's friends. In Wichita Falls, Temple hired a hack and two horses for the remaining 190 miles to Mobeetie. The honeymooners camped out each night on the prairie, and when they reached Mobeetie they were given a rousing welcome by local cowboys, who galloped past them in pairs, whooping and firing their six-guns.

Mr. and Mrs. Houston had four children. Laura was permanently captivated by her flamboyant husband, as was he by her, lavishing her with gifts throughout their marriage.

TERLINGUA
TEXAS

Many aficionados regard isolated Terlingua, located in the desert area known as Big Bend Country, as the best ghost town in the entire state of Texas.

A creek that flows into the Rio Grande was once called Tres Lenguas (Three Languages) because three tribes of American Indians—Comanches, Apaches, and Shawnees (one band somehow ventured into the Southwest)—lived along three branches of the creek.

Tres Lenguas was eventually slurred by usage into Terlingua, and a small Mexican village that grew up along the creek became known by that name.

Cowboys Jess Parker and Devine McKinney were among the first men to notice reddish outcroppings in the area while rounding up strays. By the 1880s, the soft red rock was yielding mercury through crude surface-mining methods.

Quality construction and the desert's dry climate have helped preserve this old wagon, a relic from Terlingua's earliest days.

Terlingua today, looking south. In the foreground at left is an old Catholic church. Downhill, at the center of the photo, is the old adobe school. Behind it is the two-story former headquarters of mine owner Howard Perry.

Hired and supervised by Anglo-Americans, Mexican laborers crossed the Rio Grande to work outcroppings and shallow excavations throughout the district. Dumping cinnabar ore into burro-drawn carts, they carried the ore to simple furnaces, where high temperatures vaporized the mercury. As the mercury rose to the top, it condensed into liquid form and was profitably sold as quicksilver.

These rich surface deposits were exhausted within a decade, so the laborers began to dig shafts with picks, sledgehammers, and hand drills. By the turn of the century, some of the shafts were 80 feet deep. Miners had to strap rawhide buckets filled with ore to their backs, then climb crude ladders to the surface.

Intensive development did not occur until 1903, when Howard Perry of Chicago invested heavily in a mine he named after the nearby Chisos Mountains. A town of more than 1,000 grew up around the Chisos Mining Company and was called Terlingua; the older community to the south became known as Terlingua Abaja (Lower Terlingua). Shafts were sunk as deep as 800 feet, and the Chisos Mine became one of the largest quicksilver producers in the United States.

For decades Terlingua was a classic company town. The Chisos Store was a large general store and cantina where the Mexican miners, who earned $2 per day but were far removed from any other town, spent their wages. Later the company built an adobe movie theater and installed gasoline pumps, continuing to collect all of the wages paid to the employees. An adobe Catholic church was erected, and when the community outgrew its one-room school, a four-room adobe building was constructed. A tiny jail near the theater was rarely used.

Terlingua's most impressive structure was—and remains—a two-story mine office on a hill west of the store. Residences for Anglo-American personnel were also located west of the store, while the modest adobe or stone homes of the Mexican families were to the east. A picturesque cemetery was established on the eastern outskirts of town.

During the first three decades of its existence, the Chisos Mining Company marketed an estimated $12 million worth of quicksilver, but in 1936 production began a steady decline. The company declared insolvency in 1942, and the next year the mine was sold for $81,000 to the Texas Railway Equipment Company.

After two more years of operation, the imposing mine structures were sold for salvage. By the end of the decade, Terlingua was completely deserted.

Fortunately, old buildings deteriorate slowly in the desert climate, and much of what was left still stands. The town returns to life for a few days each year when it hosts the West's most famous chili cook-off.

Above right: Hotel Chisos during Terlingua's declining years. **Bottom right:** View of Terlingua from the mine offices. The rear of the company store can be seen at far right; the Catholic church is visible at upper left.

Final rays of the setting sun bathe an abandoned furnace on the outskirts of town.

Top of page: Terlingua was unusually isolated, so a large portion of miners' salaries was spent at the company store and cantina. Eventually, the company built an adobe movie theater just north of the store. The theater has been restored for the town's annual chili cook-off. **Above:** An old rock house continues to provide shelter from the elements.

Clockwise from top left: El cemeterio, the final resting place for several generations of Terlinguans; hoist for a mine elevator; abandoned mine shaft, one of many that honeycomb the area and make it potentially hazardous for today's visitors.

ENTREPRENEUR
HOWARD PERRY

The Mexican workers at Terlingua called quiet, slightly built Howard Perry, "Chapito" (Little Man). They also called him "El Patron" (The Boss), because he owned the Chisos Mining Company, which he ran with complete authority.

Perry was born in Cleveland in 1858, and after attending Oberlin College he joined his father's lumber business. A gifted entrepreneur, Perry amassed great wealth. He moved to Chicago, married at the age of 39 (the couple had no children), and invested in the shoe manufacturing firm of his father-in-law.

In 1887, Perry purchased 2,880 acres of land in the Terlingua area for $5,760. Later he hired an attorney from Alpine, 90 miles north of Terlingua, to inspect the property.

Stimulated by the attorney's report, Perry incorporated the Chisos Mining Company in 1903 and employed Robert Lee Cartledge to manage the enterprise.

Cartledge and his administrative staff proved efficient and loyal, and the Chisos mine added millions to Perry's fortune. Perry's visits to Terlingua were infrequent, but he corresponded daily with the keepers of his profitable quicksilver mine.

In 1917, Perry moved to Portland, Maine. He died in Boston in 1944, a year after he finally sold his mine.

The home of Howard E. Perry also contained the offices of the Chisos Mining Company. Upstairs, the open dining area beneath the tile roof offered relief from the desert heat.

THE ROCKY MOUNTAINS

CRIPPLE CREEK
COLORADO

Since its first gold discovery in 1858, the state of Colorado has produced nearly a billion dollars' worth of the precious metal—approximately three percent of the world's supply. Half of that bounty came from the legendary Cripple Creek District.

Gold was discovered in the district in 1890, and during the next decade at least two dozen large-scale mines were put into operation. By the turn of the century, annual production exceeded $18 million.

The town of Cripple Creek, for which the district was named, traces its origins to 1885, when a pair of Denver real estate men, Julian Meyers and Horace Bennett, bought considerable land around what would become the town site, initially intending it as a cattle range and fishing location. When gold was discovered nearby, they decided to create a town instead, which they platted in 1891, naming

Cripple Creek today. At the turn of the century, the valley was jammed with buildings, and the population reached 25,000.

Almost all of the buildings in Cripple Creek are a century old. Commercial structures housed almost every type of business, including more than 70 saloons. Above these ground-floor enterprises were the offices of some 60 doctors and 90 lawyers.

Winter in Cripple Creek. Nov. 24th 92

Above: Cripple Creek in November of 1892 was a ramshackle boomtown, growing at a rate of 1,000 adventurers monthly by some estimates. Corner lots sold for $50, and inside lots were just $25, but real estate values soon soared. **Right:** In 1903, the mining industry was faced with one of the most violent labor wars in United States history. The army had to be called in, and a strike-related lynching occurred in 1904. **Facing page, top:** Bartenders and patrons—including a pair of lawmen (center)—at the White House Saloon in Cripple Creek, circa 1896. **Facing page, bottom:** Bennett Avenue, the main commercial street of Cripple Creek, before the fires of 1896.

Top photo: Prior to the arrival of the first rail line in the summer of 1894, the Cripple Creek District was served by several stage-coach and wagon freighting companies, including this Kuykendall Transportation Company stage. **Bottom photo:** On April 15, 1896, fire broke out in a dance hall, consuming 15 acres of Cripple Creek within a few hours. Four days later, another blaze leveled most of the rest of the city.

the principal streets Meyers and Bennett Avenues. Cripple Creek went up quickly, but two fires within a four-day period in April of 1896 wiped out most of the ramshackle city. Relief trains from nearby Colorado Springs provided thousands of homeless residents with food, blankets, and tents, and all mines were closed so that miners could help clear debris. Meanwhile, investors from near and far poured in capital for new construction.

By 1900, there were 11 towns and 55,000 people in the district. With nearly half of the area's population, Cripple Creek became the fourth largest city in Colorado.

Eight of the district's 15 newspapers were published there, and the town claimed more than 60 doctors and 90 lawyers as full-time residents. Three railroads brought as many as 58 passenger trains into Cripple Creek daily, and two electric interurban lines connected the city with other towns around the district.

Bennett Avenue boasted block after block of beautiful commercial structures. The stock

Below: After the fire, every mine was closed so that more men would be available to help clear away the debris. Fortunately, investment capital was abundant, and the flimsy structures of the mining camp were soon replaced by impressive brick buildings.

exchange was housed in a three-story masonry structure on one prominent corner. Across the street was the city's grandest building, the five-story, 150-room National Hotel, featuring a plush penthouse suite.

The Grand Opera House, located on Meyers Avenue, boasted two balconies and the finest performers and troupes of the day. Also on Meyers Avenue were most of the more than 70 saloons that served Cripple Creek, including the Bon Ton and Crapper Jack's, and an astonishing variety of brothels. The Old Homestead, just across the street from the opera house, was considered the finest.

The quality of brothels declined as Meyers Avenue stretched eastward toward Poverty Gulch, where the cheapest women could be obtained. When Cripple Creek first boomed, prostitutes openly plied their trade all over town, much to the annoyance of women shoppers and sedate businessmen. Marshal Hi Wilson soon confined such activities to Meyers Avenue, but when hatchet-carrying temperance crusader Carry Nation visited Cripple Creek, she called it "a foul cesspool."

In 1914, a journalist by the name of Julian Street published an article about Cripple Creek in *Collier's,* focusing primarily on the red-light activities of Meyers Avenue. Cripple Creek civic leaders angrily demanded a retraction, and when the magazine refused to comply, the name of Meyers Avenue was officially changed to Julian Street.

With 475 mines, the Cripple Creek District was an inevitable target of the aggressive labor organizers of the era. In 1894, the Western Federation of Miners staged a violent strike that lasted 130 days and cost the district $3 million in lost production and wages, but which won for union members a three-dollar, eight-hour workday.

In 1903 and 1904, there was an even worse labor war that wracked the district with murders and sabotage of property. When the depot at Independence was dynamited, the public finally became outraged. Soldiers arrived and arrested large numbers of agitators, but deep bitterness lingered.

By this time, gold production had begun a steady decline, and flooding had become an expensive problem in the mines. As Cripple Creek's population departed, most of the magnificent buildings were abandoned, and many—such as the National Hotel—were razed to avoid annual taxes. But two of the smaller hotels have survived, along with a number of commercial structures and churches, the high school and hospital, and even the Old Homestead itself.

Today, Cripple Creek is a lively tourist town. In 1991, when gambling was legalized, many of the old buildings were remodeled as casinos, although most true ghost town buffs would find the pre-casino Cripple Creek far more appealing.

Above left and right:
Rediscovered by tourists,
Bennett Avenue, Cripple Creek's
main business street, is thriving
again. **Left:** The Imperial
Hotel's century-old bar after a
recent restoration.

THE NAMING OF
CRIPPLE CREEK

In 1871, Levi Welty and his family moved from their ranch near Colorado Springs to the high country west of Pikes Peak. The Weltys centered their new ranch around a winding creek, and Levi and his sons George, Frank, and Alonzo began building a protective shack over the spring that fed it.

As the men toiled, a log rolled onto Frank, injuring him slightly and causing Levi to accidentally discharge his shotgun and nick himself in the hand. The commotion caused a calf to panic and break a leg, and Alonzo, who was chopping wood, cut his foot badly enough to lay him up for weeks.

Several months later, while repairing the roof over the spring house, George fell to the ground and injured his back. At about that time, the Weltys killed a bear and sent a hired hand to take some of the meat to a neighbor. The bear meat spooked the hired hand's horse, which fell on him and put him in bed for three months.

On another occasion, Levi saw a buffalo calf in his cattle herd. He dismounted and drew his revolver to shoot the calf for meat, but accidentally shot himself in the left hand, permanently paralyzing his second finger.

As the accident toll mounted, the Weltys, who apparently were not without a sense of humor, began calling their stream Cripple Creek.

During Cripple Creek's heyday, as many as 475 gold mines were operating in the district. Today, the countryside is dotted with abandoned mine buildings.

Top photo: "This is the ride that bankrupts the English language!" enthused Teddy Roosevelt after traveling by rail through the Cripple Creek District. Today, tourists can still enjoy a scenic ride on the Cripple Creek Railroad.

Bottom photo: The Old Homestead Parlor House, once considered the most luxurious house of prostitution in the tenderloin district, provides a unique museum tour. Around the turn of the century, as many as 300 prostitutes worked the various parlor houses and "cribs" along Meyers Avenue.

WINFIELD SCOTT STRATTON

The Cripple Creek District produced nearly 30 millionaires. One of the first was an eccentric misogynist named Winfield Scott Stratton.

Born in Indiana in 1848, he was raised in the midst of eight sisters by a mother whose domination was so overwhelming that he resolved at an early age to have as little as possible to do with females. He became a confirmed woman-hater in 1876, when his 17-year-old bride revealed that she was pregnant with another man's baby.

By this time, Stratton, who soon divorced, was working in Colorado Springs as a carpenter. For 17 years he used his earnings to finance summer prospecting expeditions, but every one of his ventures was a bust—until he struck it rich with his Independence Mine, three miles southeast of Cripple

Winfield Scott Stratton was a skilled carpenter whose earnings financed his prospecting activities. At Cripple Creek he became a multimillionaire and a philanthropist.

Creek. Stratton mined $4 million worth of gold from the Independence, then sold out to a London company for $11 million. In the meantime, millions more began to accumulate from other mining investments around the district.

At the age of 48, Stratton leased a luxury suite in the new National Hotel for 50 years, but he preferred to live in his old miner's shack overlooking the nearby town of Victor. He invested in Cripple Creek's first railroad and in a myriad of mining and construction projects. He also bought the Colorado Springs streetcar company for $500,000 and improved it at a cost of $1.5 million.

His greatest pleasure, however, was philanthropy. He once gave a bicycle to every laundry woman in Colorado Springs, and he made a habit of supplying poor people with coal during the winters. He regularly grubstaked old friends, and he donated thousands of dollars to the churches of Cripple Creek.

Stratton once gave $85,000 to the Salvation Army, and when Cripple Creek was leveled by fire in 1896, he immediately organized relief trains and personally paid for the supplies from Colorado Springs merchants. One Christmas he gave $50,000 to each of his key employees, and houses to six other valued workers.

When he died in 1902, of liver failure and diabetes, Stratton left $6 million to establish and maintain a home for poor children and the elderly.

LEADVILLE
COLORADO

During the early 1860s, miners extracted more than $5 million worth of gold from California Gulch, near the future site of Leadville. More than a decade later, prospector Will Stevens tried to rework an old field, only instead of gold he found immense beds of iron carbonate rich in silver deposits. Later, the Leadville District would also yield generous amounts of lead, copper, iron, zinc, bismuth, manganese, and molybdenum.

By 1877, the rush was on, and the future silver capital of America—and one of the wickedest cities in the West—was founded on a bleak hillside at the dizzying height of 10,188 feet.

Prospectors crossed over the Continental Divide by the hundreds. Drawn by the possibility of fabulous wealth, they ignored the deadly toll exacted by the unusually high altitude, fierce winter conditions, and initial lack of food and shelter. Eventually, Leadville

Leadville in the 1890s offered 118 gambling halls, countless brothels, and more than 100 saloons.

created a succession of millionaires, including walrus-mustached H.A.W. Tabor, who poured much of his fortune back into the town. His most lasting monument was the Tabor Opera House, a magnificent structure built in 1879 and still toured by admiring visitors.

The Denver & Rio Grande Railroad reached Leadville in 1880, and soon the boomtown was bursting with nearly 40,000 citizens. Before long, the mining payroll soared to $800,000 per month. At its peak, the most renowned mine, the Robert E. Lee, produced more than $100,000 worth of minerals in a single day.

During Leadville's frenzied expansion, building sites were contested by "lot jumpers," the equivalent of claim jumpers at mining sites. Accommodations included countless shanties with log walls and canvas roofs, tent lodgings that provided mattresses and covers, and boarding houses that rented cots in eight-hour shifts. The best hotel, the three-story Tabor Grand, opened in 1885 and still stands on Harrison Avenue.

Leadville boasted almost every type of business, including seven banks and three newspapers, plus several schools and hospitals and at least seven churches. There also were more than 100 saloons and 118 gambling halls, primarily located on Chestnut and State Streets.

While famous entertainers such as Maurice Barrymore (the English-born father of American acting legends Lionel, Ethel, and John), Eddie Foy, and Oscar Wilde appeared at the Grand Central Theatre and the Tabor Opera House, such establishments as the Coliseum, Athenaeum, and the Elm Street Ring catered to those who preferred dog fights and boxing matches.

Houses of prostitution were clustered on Stillborn Alley, State Street, Lafayette Avenue, and Tiger Alley. The men who visited these infamous thoroughfares were advised to walk in the middle of the street, with gun in hand.

For gamblers there was perhaps no better play anywhere in the West than in Leadville, and the steady stream of gunmen-gamblers who came to try their luck included Ben Thompson, Bat Masterson, Luke Short, and Doc Holliday.

Leadville's incredible prosperity and exuberant lifestyle continued until the devaluation of silver in 1893, but there were so many different metals in the area that mining activities never halted.

During Prohibition, Leadville's rebellious nature reasserted itself, as the production of bootleg whiskey became a major local industry. Mines were an ideal location for stills, and more than a few miners began adding copper tubing and sugar to their shopping lists.

Bootlegging wasn't limited to miners. A local taxi service that did everything it could to discourage customers was actually a front for a bootlegging operation, and more than one of the town's soft-drink parlors dispensed "hard" drinks as well.

During World War II, a nearby Army camp for ski troops reawakened Leadville's bars and brothels, but the base was dismantled after hostilities ended. Today, tourists still come to see the frontier landmarks of the famed silver capital.

Left: The hugely successful "Little Jonny" mine in 1907. Above: Doc Holliday, notorious gunman-gambler-dentist, wounded his last victim in Leadville in 1884. Below left: The Tabor Grand Hotel, one of several architectural projects initiated by local millionaire H.A.W. Tabor. Below: Gambler Luke Short engaged in his first gunfight in Leadville in 1879.

THE RISE AND FALL OF
H.A.W. TABOR

Few Western stories are more captivating than the spectacular rise and fall of H.A.W. Tabor and his lover, Baby Doe.

Horace Austin Warner Tabor was born in Vermont in 1830, but when he was 25, the ambitious stonecutter headed West, eventually winning election to the Kansas legislature. In 1857, he married a native New Englander, the dour but industrious Augusta Pierce. Tabor soon sought his fortune in Colorado, hauling Augusta and their infant son into frigid, forbidding gold country.

Two decades passed, as Tabor became a successful merchant who supplemented his income with poker and modest mining investments. After a $17 grubstake to a pair of prospectors produced a one-third interest in the Little Pittsburg bonanza near Leadville, Tabor poured his profits into one silver strike after another.

From silk nightshirts with diamond buttons to magnificent opera houses in Leadville and Denver, the new multimillionaire spent money as fast as he made it. Tabor was elected Colorado's lieutenant governor and was later appointed to an unexpired term in the U.S. Senate. However, his political career was soon sidetracked by romantic scandal. At Leadville's posh Saddle Rock Cafe, the 50-year-old multimillionaire met Baby Doe, a lovely 26-year-old divorcee. The austere and aging Augusta, who disapproved of Tabor's lavish lifestyle, was promptly divorced with a $300,000 settlement.

In a splendid ceremony held in Washington, D.C., in 1883, Baby Doe married

Tabor, who adorned his bride with a $7,000 wedding dress and a $90,000 diamond necklace.

Baby Doe presented her adoring husband with two daughters, and she spent Horace's money as extravagantly on them as on herself. Unfortunately, Horace eventually lost his fortune in a series of harebrained investment schemes. He died almost penniless in 1899, retaining just one mining property and exhorting Baby Doe to "hang on to the Matchless."

She moved to a shack near the entrance to the mine, near Leadville, and spent the rest of her life trying to locate new paydirt. Dressed in rags, the 81-year-old Baby Doe Tabor was found frozen to death in 1935.

Top left: Frame house built by H.A.W. Tabor in 1877, before he struck it rich. **Top right:** Interior of the Tabor residence. **Bottom left:** Showing its age today, the Tabor Opera House once featured the most famous performers of its era. **Bottom right:** Tourists inspect the stage at the historic theater. **Following page:** Leadville under a fresh winter snow.

Top photo: Remains of an old mine building in view of Mt. Elbert, Colorado's highest peak (14,433 feet). Leadville's first notable mine was the Little Pittsburg; the most productive was the Robert E. Lee; and the most famous, H.A.W. Tabor's Matchless. By 1880, the monthly mining payroll in the district had soared past $800,000.
Bottom photo: The Climax Molybdenum mine, now inactive.

Top photo: Suiting the area's frontier image, dogsledding has become one of Leadville's popular winter activities. **Bottom photo:** Boasting a superb collection of historic Victorian structures, plus an ample selection of restaurants, stores, and hotels, modern Leadville relies heavily on tourism.

CENTRAL CITY
COLORADO

"**G**o West, young man, go West." Throughout the 1850s, Horace Greeley, respected editor of the *New York Tribune,* preached his famous theme to adventurous Americans. Among the multitudes who heeded Greeley's advice was John H. Gregory, who left Georgia in 1858 with the intention of working his way to the California gold fields.

Along the way, Gregory gravitated to Cherry Creek in the Colorado Territory, where gold had just been discovered at the future site of Denver. Heeding the speculation of veteran prospectors who suspected the source was in the mountains to the west, Gregory braved frigid winter conditions and altitudes of 8,500 feet, finally locating gold in a precipitous canyon in May of 1859.

Prospectors rushed to "Gregory Gulch" by the thousands, and even Greeley himself appeared, in the midst of a long-planned trip to California. The 48-year-old Greeley rode a mule into Gregory Gulch,

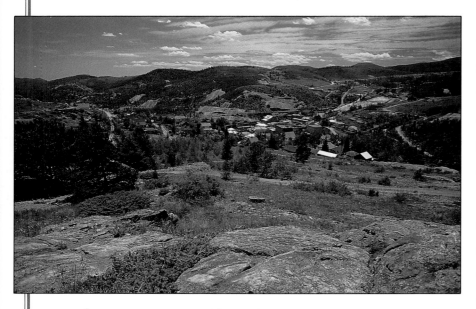

Contemporary overview of Central City. During its heyday, the town was known as "the richest square mile on Earth."

Looking down Central City's picturesque Main Street, which dead-ends at historic Eureka Street. Beyond the well-preserved commercial district, private residences climb the slopes of the surrounding hillsides.

kling and Co., and miners banded together to purchase mills of 5, 10, or 15 stamps. Soon, more than 100 stamp mills were noisily crushing ore. The area was denuded as trees were cut down for buildings, fuel, and mine supports.

Mining camps stretched for miles through winding Gregory Gulch, but the middle camp quickly became the most prominent. At first known as Mountain City, the name was changed to Central City because of its central location. Boasting that it was built astride "the richest square mile in the world," Central City boomed for a time into Colorado's largest municipality. For a while, it even rivaled Denver as a site for the capital.

One of the renowned actors of the time, Jack Langrishe, installed his company for three months in the Montana Theater. A sprawling two-story log structure, the theater downstairs had a barber shop, bar, and store, while the upstairs loft was lit with candles and outfitted with chairs.

Langrishe offered burlesque and melodrama, eventually discovering the bawdy comedy talents of a drunken miner named Mike Dougherty, who cut his performing career short by drinking himself to death within a few years. Another performer was billed as "Mlle. Rose Haydee." The "mademoiselle" actually was from Missouri, but exotic pretensions were lost on the miners, who thought her name was "Millie."

Prosperity continued through the 1870s and into the 1880s. A railroad reached Black Hawk, 500 feet below Central City, in 1872, but it was 1878 before Chinese laborers could complete the 3½ miles of loops and trestles to Central City.

where he observed at least 10,000 men furiously working their claims. At night, he noted the glow of campfires stretching for miles, because at this early stage, many men did not yet have cabins or even tents, having no choice but to huddle around fires during the cold nights.

The famous journalist was escorted to a sandbar that the miners had just "salted" by shooting large quantities of gold dust into it with a shotgun. The miners gave Greeley a pan and instructions, and he was elated over the spectacular results. "Gentlemen," Greeley exclaimed, "I have washed with my very own hands and seen with my own eyes, and the news of your rich discovery shall go forth over all the world as far as my newspaper can carry it."

Greeley's favorable reports contributed to boom conditions in Gregory Gulch. Within a year the surface gold was panned out, but Colorado's first quartz mill was brought in by Prosser, Con-

In 1874, a fire started in the house of a Chinese resident who was burning incense, and within several hours most of Central City had been leveled. But the boomtown quickly rebuilt in brick and stone. Cornishmen who had emigrated to find employment in the mines lent their skills as masons to the reconstruction, and much of their fine masonry work may still be admired. The Cornishmen added a unique flavor to Central City, singing songs of their homeland as they marched to and from work.

Perhaps the most impressive structure to rise from the ashes was the Central City Opera House, which showcased Sarah Bernhardt, Edwin Booth, Lotta Crabtree, and other notables of the stage.

Although the initial success of the Opera House lasted only a few years, the magnificent old theater was responsible for an annual revival during Central City's most somnolent period.

By the early 20th century, the mines were depleted and Central City was a shadow of its former self. But in the summer of 1932, during the heart of the Great Depression, the Opera House was reopened for a two-week run of *Camille,* starring Lillian Gish. The summer theater festival became a popular annual event.

A devastating blaze on May 21, 1874, destroyed most of Central City. One of the few structures left standing was the stone Wells Fargo office (foreground). Despite the massive destruction, the boomtown was quickly rebuilt.

The Opera House featured such giants of the American stage as Edwin Booth and Sarah Bernhardt.

The Central City Opera House, built at a cost of $25,000, opened in March of 1878. The balcony was reserved for miners, who often tromped to performances straight from the mines.

Top photo: Buildings erected more than a century ago can still be found along the now quiet streets of Central City.

Bottom photo: Three more Eureka Street landmarks: the Williams Stables, City Hall (with a fire bell atop the roof), and St. James M. E. Church, founded by missionaries within a year after prospectors first came to the mining camp.

The economy of Central City has been rejuvenated in recent years with the introduction of casino gambling.

THE REMARKABLE
TELLER HOUSE

For more than a decade, Central City lacked a first-class hotel. In December of 1868, two prosperous citizens pledged $3,000 toward building one, triggering a community-wide drive to raise $10,000.

The amount had not quite been reached by 1871, when Henry M. Teller, president of the Colorado Central Railroad that would soon reach nearby Black Hawk, offered $30,000 if the populace would provide $25,000. Within three days the money had been pledged, and ground was broken in July of 1871.

A year later the Teller House opened with an eight-course banquet and a grand ball that lasted until dawn. Visitors admired the hotel's ornate parlors, a dining room that could accommodate nearly 200, an enormous cooking range that looked like a

Central City's historic Teller House hotel and casino.

narrow-gauge locomotive, a reading room, and a splendid barroom with billiard tables.

One observer approved of the lack of transoms: "Guests may therefore lie down to peaceful slumbers undisturbed by apprehensions of getting their heads blown off or valuables lifted by burglars."

For its first New Year's dinner, the Teller House promised "the most elaborate bill of fare" ever offered by a Western hotel, and it may very well have succeeded. The menu included an incredible array of fish, beef, veal, mutton, pork, turkey, mallard duck, mountain grouse, prairie chicken, wild turkey, antelope, venison, buffalo, and Rocky Mountain black bear, with a full complement of vegetables, relishes, and other side dishes, plus pastries, puddings, ice cream, and a pyramid of cakes.

H.A.W. Tabor was only one of many mining millionaires to stay in the Teller House. Governor John Evans spent $20,000 to furnish the front suite that he claimed as his own; other distinguished guests included poet Walt Whitman and President Ulysses S. Grant. Their rooms may be visited today by any history-minded tourist who wants to step inside this superbly preserved relic.

Top photo: Lobby of the Teller House in 1901. The cases along the right wall displayed a fine collection of minerals and and other geological specimens. Adjoining the lobby were a library, barber shop, billiard room, and bar. **Bottom photo:** One of the hotel's parlor rooms.

115

CREEDE
COLORADO

"**Y**ou couldn't sleep with all the noise," complained an overnight visitor to a Creede hotel more than a century ago. "All night long there was hollering, yelling, horses galloping, wagons chuckling, pounding, sawing, shooting."

During its three raucous years as a silver-mining boomtown, Creede teemed with prospectors, gamblers, prostitutes, and frontier adventurers of every type. The Colorado town attracted such notables as Bat Masterson, Calamity Jane, "Soapy" Smith (the West's premier con man), and cigar-smoking Poker Alice Tubbs.

"Creede is unfortunate in getting more of the flotsam of the state than usually falls to the lot of mining camps," complained the town's newspaper, the *Creede Candle.* "Some of her citizens would take grubstake prize at a hog show."

In recent years, Creede has developed into a popular resort center.

Creede's business district was jammed into a gorge, but log and frame residences were built on a mesa above town. As Creede boomed during the 1890s, carpenters worked night and day to keep up with the housing demand.

The last great silver boom was initiated by prospector Nicholas C. Creede, who discovered paydirt in 1889 in rugged Willow Creek Canyon. Creede was soon bought out by three financiers who hired him to locate more mines. His successful efforts were carried out with maximum possible secrecy, but by 1890, word of the new strike had spread. The boom was on.

Located near the headwaters of the Rio Grande in the towering San Juan Mountains, the camp was called Willow and Jimtown (and Gintown, because of the constant consumption of the lethal beverage), but was finally named Creede.

Within a year, 10,000 fortune-seekers jammed the narrow canyon. Shacks were built up the sides of the surrounding mountains, sometimes with cliffs serving as rear walls, and a number of privies were perched directly over the creek.

Nicer residences began to be erected on Capitol Hill, the mesa overlooking the gulch. As tents gave way to frame structures, 200 carpenters worked night and day, as did gamblers, bartenders, and prostitutes.

After sunset, illumination was provided by huge flares placed throughout the town. Later, an electric plant was hastily constructed, and lights blazed from dusk until dawn.

Nicholas C. Creede

Miners looking for fun—or trouble—could find both in Creede's lively business district, photographed on June 1, 1892.

Space in rooming houses was reserved well before construction began, and newcomers were hard-pressed to find decent lodgings. One grandly named hotel, The Palace, was nothing more than a board shanty sixteen feet square with a blanket for a door. Such crude hostelries generally had 20 to 60 cots in a room, with a charge of one dollar per night with blankets and 50 cents without.

Late in 1891, a long awaited branch of the Denver and Rio Grande Railroad reached Creede. Any Pullman cars that came into town were immediately put into service as temporary hotels.

Horse-drawn ore sleds and heavily laden burro trains streamed into the railroad depot to unload tons of ore, while two daily passenger trains brought in as many as 300 new citizens, many of them sitting on each other. Freight trains unloaded piles of packing cases, barrels, supply boxes, beer kegs, furniture, and cast-iron stoves before loading up with ore.

The whiskey supply was adequate, but was routinely stretched by adding grain alcohol and distilled water—and two plugs of tobacco—to each barrel. The price was $1 per shot at more than 30 saloons.

Creede in 1945. With many of its citizens involved in the war effort, the population sagged to 500, and many buildings stood empty.

Above: Bob Ford, who murdered Jesse James in 1882, ran a tent saloon during Creede's boom period. On June 8, 1892, a dispute with a patron led to gunplay, and Ford was killed by a slug that drove his collar button through his throat. **Above right:** Ford's funeral on Shotgun Hill. His remains were later moved by his family to Richmond, Missouri.

Creede's first church service, it turns out, was held in a saloon—actually a tent, but a saloon nonetheless. The congregation was happy to secure a place for Easter services, but some members were dismayed when they learned that a prizefight was scheduled right behind them.

Bob Ford, killer of Jesse James, operated a saloon in a tent until June 8, 1892, when Ed O. Kelly did him in with a shotgun blast. Guzzling liquor all the way, a huge crowd accompanied Ford's corpse to Creede's appropriately named Shotgun Hill, where numerous other shooting victims had been laid to rest.

Three days before Ford was slain, fire started in a saloon and raged through the heart of Creede, destroying many buildings and even a dozen bridges that spanned narrow Willow Creek. The town quickly rebuilt, however, and the next year became the seat of newly created Mineral County.

In 1893, silver was devalued by the government, and even though gold and zinc were also produced by Creede's mines, the town's population began to drop—as if residents could sense that change was on the way.

Soon, the rowdy era was over, and Creede was in sharp decline by the turn of the century. But mine production never ceased, and tourists, particularly hunters and anglers, still flock to what remains of Creede every summer.

Top photo: Cigar-smoking Poker Alice Tubbs, a noted frontier gambler, shown here in old age.
Above: Jefferson Randolph "Soapy" Smith, the West's premier con man.

A ramshackle remnant of the Commodore Mine. During Creede's boom, houses and even privies were routinely built against even the steepest mountainsides.

Top photo: Contemporary view of Creede's main street, a much quieter thoroughfare than it was a century ago.

Bottom photo: Creede was a regular stop for traveling entertainers of the 1890s. Today the Creede Opera House continues to stage performances for tourists.

Left: Tourists enjoy quaint shops in downtown Creede.
Above: Creede sprang up during the height of Victorian architecture, when carpenters routinely used jigsaws to add Gingerbread and other decorative features to homes.

Still serving the public, Creede's old fire station has been converted into a charming restaurant and bed-and-breakfast.

Enjoying a bit of history with their sport, local cyclists routinely include abandoned mines on their freewheeling itineraries.

THE PRANK OF THE
PARSON'S PANTS

Late in 1891, Bat Masterson was hired as gambling manager of Creede's popular Denver Exchange. The big saloon-restaurant-gambling hall ran 24 hours a day, taking in an average of $650 in daily bar receipts alone. Almost every known gambling device was installed, and Bat was usually working the floor 16 hours each day.

One night Bat was approached by Parson Tom Uzzell, asking for an opportunity to preach, as he had routinely done in numerous mining camps. With misgivings (which proved to be correct) that a sermon would dampen play, Bat banged a whiskey bottle on the bar and asked everyone to remove their hats while Parson Tom preached.

The sermon was about the Prodigal Son, and when one gambler asked another what he thought of

William Barclay "Bat" Masterson had a reputation as a gambler and gunfighter, but he was also a notorious practical joker.

the story, he replied, "I think that the fatted calf got a damned bad break."

Bat directed a bartender to pass a hat, and Parson Tom left the Denver Exchange gratefully announcing that the collection would be used to build a church in Creede. A short time later, several of the gamblers proclaimed a desire to double Parson Tom's church money, but no one knew how much had been collected.

It was then that Bat, a notorious practical joker, dispatched three of con man "Soapy" Smith's henchmen to steal Parson Tom's pants while he slept in a tent. When they returned, the silver-laden pockets were emptied and $346 was tallied. The men chipped in enough to make the total an even $700, and Bat locked the pants in a saloon safe.

At dawn, Parson Tom roared into the saloon clad in his red longjohns and knee boots, calling for God to strike down the thief who had stolen his pants and money. The saloon's assemblage suddenly burst into laughter, whereupon Bat produced the pants and the missing funds. Honoring the tradition of big winners, Parson Tom bought a round of drinks for all, and the prank became part of Colorado's frontier folklore.

SOUTH PASS CITY
WYOMING

Mountain men began to cross the Continental Divide at South Pass, Wyoming, more than 7,800 feet above sea level, as early as 1812. The ensuing years would bring thousands of emigrants across the Pass, many of them bound for Oregon. Beginning in 1849, however, traffic increased substantially as countless waves of gold-seekers flowed through South Pass en route to California.

Traces of gold were found in this busy region as early as 1842, and by the early 1860s prospectors were panning throughout the area. Paydirt was found along Willow Creek in 1867, and the inevitable rush that followed produced a mining camp called South Pass City some 15 miles northeast of the Pass.

Real estate promoters aggressively built commercial structures in South Pass City and, five miles to the northeast, in Atlantic City. These one-story buildings were of log construction with decorative false fronts made of planks.

South Pass City used to be Wyoming's largest town. Back in 1870, several hundred buildings occupied the site, and the town's population reached 4,000.

The uppermost reaches of the famous Carissa Mine overlooked the entire valley. Prospectors found gold "in paying quantities" here in 1867.

Indian raids scattered many of the prospectors, while other miners hired on with Union Pacific construction crews that were working in the vicinity. When early traveler James Chisholm arrived in South Pass City in September of 1868, he found most of the new buildings unoccupied, noting: "The actual number of residents number not over 50 or 60."

By the next year, however, investors were developing mines near South Pass City and Atlantic City. The biggest producer was the Carissa Mine, located on a hill just above and to the north of South Pass City.

With mining payrolls available, along with abundant paydirt for profitable panning, the population boomed. Although the census of 1870 found only 9,118 non-Indians residing in Wyoming, South Pass City was the territory's largest town, with a population estimated at 4,000.

Main Street was half a mile long, paralleling Willow Creek, and there were two principal cross streets. The town had a bank, a newspaper, several inns, a school, a jail, several general stores, and a millinery shop.

The Keg, Fatty's Place, the 49er, the Elephant, the Occidental, Gilman's, and other saloons provided endless opportunities for drinking and gambling. Other recreation was offered by a bowling alley, a shooting gallery—and the inevitable bordellos.

The town experienced relatively little violence, and the town's two doctors spent as much time trying to develop their claims as they did in their offices. The usual litigation over mining claims kept four law firms busy.

But not for long. Placer mining soon became unprofitable, and the Carissa and other mines gradually exhausted their veins during the 1870s. The seat of vast Carter County was moved to Green River, and by 1880, South Pass City was virtually deserted.

Many of the buildings were moved or dismantled for their materials, but the remaining structures of the ghost town are maintained as a state historic site.

The miner at left is using a star drill and hammer to make a hole for an explosive charge. Miners typically worked 12-hour shifts by candlelight. Child labor laws were not yet in effect, and there were no hard hats or other safety measures for the protection of workers.

Above: South Pass City in 1904. A thriving gold-mining center in the late 1860s and 1870s, the town started to decline when placer mining became unprofitable.

Left: Members of the Rock Springs (Wyoming) Band pose in front of the Sherlock Hotel in June of 1894. The band had been "imported" to entertain prospective gold mine investors.

Top Left: Ruins of South Pass City jail. **Top right:** Front desk in the lobby of the Sherlock Hotel. **Below:** The town is maintained as a state historic site. The building closest to the camera is the Sherlock Hotel. Next to it is an old dining hall, and beyond that, the express office.

Typical of boomtown architecture, South Pass City's general store was a simple log structure with a false front made of planks.

JUSTICE OF THE PEACE
ESTHER MORRIS

The first legislation granting American women the right to vote was passed in 1869 in the Wyoming Territory. The struggle earned South Pass City resident Esther Mc-Quigg Morris the sobriquet "Mother of Woman's Suffrage in Wyoming."

Orphaned as a child, Morris had made a small fortune in business, but when her husband died in Illinois, she was harmed financially by unjust property laws. When she left for South Pass City in 1869 to join her second husband, a merchant, her brother declared, "You will never live to see the day women vote."

The first legislature of the new territory was about to meet in Cheyenne. In South Pass City, Esther held a historic tea party for legislative candidates, extracting promises that the winners would introduce a bill giving women the right to vote and hold office. William Bright won, and he introduced the bill in Cheyenne. When the bill passed, unenfranchised women around the United States—and the world—were enormously encouraged.

Esther Morris then received an appointment as the first female justice of the peace, taking office in South Pass City early in 1870. Newspaper correspondents from across the country were sent to interview her, and she was besieged with speaking invitations. She counseled suffragettes not to agitate: "The women can do nothing without the help of the men."

Judge Morris handled 34 cases with general approval before stepping down from her post in November of 1870.

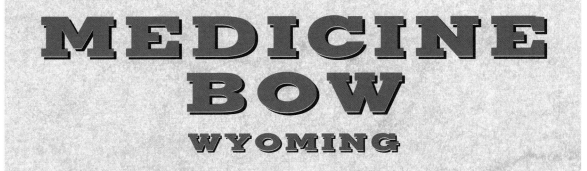

MEDICINE BOW
WYOMING

When the Union Pacific Railroad was expanding westward across the vast plains of Wyoming in 1868, a pumping station to provide water for engines was erected beside the Medicine Bow River.

The river and surrounding mountains had been named by Indians, who annually trekked to the forests at the base of the mountains to make their bows from ash trees. Indians used the term "good medicine" to describe things that were ideal for their given purpose, and so the site became known as the place where warriors could obtain "good medicine" bows.

Within a few years, open-range cattle ranching was introduced to the Medicine Bow region, and stockyards were built near the station. When Medicine Bow became a shipping point, a couple of saloons went up to serve the cowboys. Soon there was a general store and a small hotel, and meals were served at the U.P. section house.

View of Virginian Hotel and other historic buildings in Medicine Bow.

Union Pacific Railroad depot in Medicine Bow, built in 1913 after the original station burned down. The railroad closed the depot in 1981, after which it was placed on the National Register of Historic Places and reopened as a museum.

The saloons and eateries of Medicine Bow were patronized by "tie hacks," who were employed at a camp in the nearby mountains. These rugged lumberjacks cut hundreds of thousands of railroad ties and mining timbers, floating them downriver to a boom a mile above Medicine Bow. A number of other men worked at the boom to pull the timber pieces ashore. These tie hacks joined cowboys at the bars of Medicine Bow, and they were as rough and rowdy as any of them.

Twice during the early years of Medicine Bow, the little village was attacked by Indian war parties. One assault was quickly dispersed, but another siege had to be relieved by a column from Fort Fred Steele. A military substation at Medicine Bow temporarily provided protection from Indian attack.

A school was built in 1876, and within a few more years, Medicine Bow was the largest shipping point on the Union Pacific line. Later, sheep-raising became a major Wyoming range industry, and by the turn of the century, Medicine Bow shipped 1,000 tons of wool annually.

By that time, too, Owen Wister had begun to visit the town to gather material for his Western short stories and novels. When *The Virginian* was released in 1902, Medicine Bow was mentioned throughout the book.

Following a long absence, Wister returned to Medicine Bow on a family vacation in 1911. The next year, the author bought a small ranch in the area, but he never came back. His wife died in Rhode Island while giving birth to their sixth child, and Wister sold the ranch in 1920. The cabin he built was restored and put on display in Medicine Bow in 1994.

The Union Pacific transferred ownership of the town site to Medicine Bow in 1909, and the community was incorporated. That same year, construction was begun on the three-story Virginian Hotel, which opened in 1911 with a banquet and all-night ball. Paintings by renowned Western artist Charles Russell decorated the lobby. The Virginian Hotel was renovated and restored in 1984, and today provides part of the exhilarating Western atmosphere in the small town natives call "the Bow."

"The Wild Bunch" (shown here in a famous photo taken in December of 1900) passed through Medicine Bow during the summer of 1899. Seated, left to right: Harry Longabaugh (The Sundance Kid), Ben Kilpatrick, Robert Leroy Parker (Butch Cassidy). Standing, left to right: Will Carver and the murderous Harvey Logan (Kid Curry).

Top photo: A couple of hours after midnight on June 2, 1899, a Union Pacific train headed toward Medicine Bow was robbed by Butch Cassidy's "Wild Bunch." The train was intercepted near Wilcox, a whistle stop 15 miles southeast of Medicine Bow. The gang blew the express car apart with a dynamite charge so powerful that debris was scattered for 100 feet in every direction. **Bottom photo:** Posse assigned to track down the Wild Bunch: George Hiatt (1), T. T. Kelliher (2), Joe LeFors (3), H. Davis (4), Si Funk (5), and Jeff Carr (6).

Above: A weathered old wagon decorates the boardwalk outside the Virginian Hotel.
Right: Inside the lobby of the Virginian. In 1909 August Grimm, the first mayor of Medicine Bow, and his partner, George Plummer, began construction of the hotel named after Owen Wister's famous novel. The Grand Opening of the three-story hostelry was held on September 30, 1911.

The dining room of the Virginian received special attention during the hotel's 1984 renovation.

Right: The Medicine Bow State Bank was built in 1911. Eight years later, it was purchased by a group of ranchers and renamed the Stockman's State Bank. **Below:** In 1912, novelist Owen Wister purchased a small Wyoming ranch and arranged for a log cabin to be built for his family. When his wife died during childbirth, Wister lost interest in the property, which was eventually donated to Grand Teton National Park. Dismantled and stored for safekeeping, the cabin was only recently reassembled, becoming part of the Medicine Bow Museum in 1994.

WESTERN NOVELIST
OWEN WISTER

"When you call me that, smile!"

The famous expression first appeared in Owen Wister's acclaimed novel, *The Virginian.* Citizens of Medicine Bow remain proud that much of the background material for this landmark work of fiction was acquired by Wister in their town.

The only child of a cultured Eastern family, Wister was born in 1860 and educated at exclusive schools abroad and in New England. Between 1885 and 1914, he made 15 trips to the West, often staying as long as six months. From the very beginning, Wister was fascinated by Western people, terrain, and wildlife. "Why wasn't some Kipling saving the sagebrush for American literature?" he mused in 1891.

Wister published the first of more than 70 Western short stories within the year. In an enviable stroke of good fortune, he obtained a position with Francis Rawle, a successful attorney who, in the spirit of Renaissance patrons, maintained Wister in his prestigious law office, "where I worked at fiction for twenty-five years, and at law nevermore."

Wister's masterpiece, dedicated to friend and Harvard classmate Theodore Roosevelt, was published in 1902 and became an immediate bestseller. Curiously, the man who revealed the enormous appeal of the cowboy story to adult audiences never wrote another Western novel. He died in Rhode Island in 1938.

Above: Owen Wister (1860–1938) was 25 when he first arrived in Medicine Bow. He slept on the long counter of the frontier town's general store. **Left:** Wister's most famous book, *The Virginian,* was published in 1902 and dedicated to his friend, Theodore Roosevelt. An immediate sensation, *The Virginian* became a Broadway play, was produced four times as a motion picture, and was the basis of a popular television series.

VIRGINIA CITY
MONTANA

After gold began to flow from a Montana mining camp called Bannack City in 1862, hundreds of prospectors swarmed to the site. Others, like Bill Fairweather, ventured into the neighboring mountains.

Fairweather led five other miners into Alder Gulch, a tributary of the Gallatin River. In May of 1862, the men discovered paydirt, and after panning gold for a couple of days, they left to buy supplies at Bannack, 70 miles away.

Although intending to keep their strike secret, the information leaked out, and when Fairweather and his partners returned to their claim, they were accompanied by a horde of other prospectors.

The camp that sprang up was called Varina by Confederate sympathizers, in honor of the wife of Jefferson Davis. Unionists objected to the name, but a compromise was reached, and the name was changed to Virginia City (which caused considerable confusion with Easterners unfamiliar with the geography of the West, since

Virginia City sprang up quickly in Montana's gold-rich Alder Gulch.

Looking south at Virginia City. The center of town is dominated by the impressive Madison County courthouse, begun in 1875. To the left is St. Paul's Episcopal Church, a stone building erected in 1902 to replace the 1868 frame structure.

Virginia City, Nevada, had been settled four years earlier).

Within a year, Virginia City's population was up to 4,000, with thousands more in Nevada City and other nearby boomtowns. During that period, $10 million worth of gold dust and nuggets was found in Alder Gulch, and $20 million more was mined during the next four years.

In May of 1864, the United States Congress, responding to petitions circulated among the mining camps, created the Territory of Montana. The following December the territorial legislature, meeting in Bannack, selected Virginia City as the territorial capital, convening there the following February.

The capital city's population rollicked in scores of saloons, gambling halls, bawdy houses, billiard parlors, opium dens, and various other centers of masculine amusement. From the earliest days of the Alder Gulch rush, there was a degree of criminal activity unusual even for a frontier mining town. Murder, robbery, and claim jumping were so rampant that in December of 1863, a vigilance committee pledged itself "to the laudible purpos of arresting thieves & murderers & recovering stollen property...." [sic].

By this time there had been more than 100 murders in the vicinity, and the vigilantes responded by lynching nearly 30 criminals. On January 14, 1864, the vicious killer Boone Helm and

Below: The stone Creighton block still stands on the south side of Wallace Street, Virginia City's main thoroughfare.

Left: Chinese general store, on the north side of Wallace Street, around the turn of the century. **Below:** Content Corner was built for Soloman P. Content on the south side of Wallace Street at the intersection of Jackson. When completed in September of 1864, it was Virginia City's most impressive business structure, and for a time the upstairs housed offices of the territorial government. Robert Vickers bought the building in 1883 and in 1895 extensively remodeled the front, altering the pointed gothic window arches and installing plate glass for merchandise displays.

four other desperadoes were hanged in an unfinished building. Ropes were dropped over the ceiling rafters, and the badmen were hoisted up to strangle to death.

Another famous Virginia City execution was carried out the following March. Jack Slade had established a notorious reputation before coming to Virginia City, where he tried to start a ranch. But Slade was plagued by alcoholism, and after a particularly troublesome saloon quarrel he was dragged outside and hanged from a beam. "My God! My God!" cried Slade. "Must I die like this? Oh, my poor wife!"

His poor wife sealed the corpse inside a tin coffin filled with raw alcohol, traveling as far as Salt Lake City before the cargo became so odorous that it had to be buried in a Mormon Cemetery—more than four months after the lynching.

A somewhat more tranquil Virginia City soon boasted Methodist, Episcopal, and Catholic churches, as well as a Masonic Lodge. Most of the principal buildings lined mile-long Wallace Street, a 75-foot-wide, east-west thoroughfare that paralleled Daylight Creek.

The town had a handsome courthouse and several good hotels, but the proposed capitol building was never erected. It was just as well; gold production soon slowed in Alder Gulch, and in 1875, the territorial capital was moved to a more promising mining town, Helena.

Even though the population declined, Virginia City maintained itself as an outfitting point for tourists heading to Yellowstone National Park and as a business center for area ranches. Today, tourists still flock to Virginia City to enjoy its lively Old West atmosphere.

Left: Thompson Hickman Memorial Library and Museum on Wallace Street.
Below Left: William H. "Bill" Fairweather led the prospecting company that discovered gold in Alder Gulch. He died in 1875 at the age of 39 and was buried in Virginia City's new cemetery on a hill overlooking Alder Gulch.
Below: The Fairweather Inn originally was the Anaconda Hotel. It boasted a restaurant, a barroom with billiard tables, a bowling alley in the basement, and a rear entrance for ladies of the night. Remodeled in the 1930s, the old hotel became the Fairweather Inn a decade later.

Original Virginia City storefronts. In 1945, Charles and Sue Bovey visited Virginia City and were impressed by the large number of original buildings still standing. The Boveys resourcefully began a long-range restoration project, also acquiring numerous authentic structures to reconstruct nearby Nevada City.

As part of their restoration project, Charles and Sue Bovey restocked the old stores with period merchandise. Many interiors were arranged by Zena Hoff, who was born in Denmark in 1889 but settled in Virginia City during the 1930s.

Top photo: The restoration of Virginia City is an ongoing project that was started half a century ago. The population had dropped below 200, but unused, deteriorating structures were gradually restored to support a growing tourist trade. Several 19th-century buildings were brought here from other locations in Montana, while others were rebuilt to historically accurate specifications. **Bottom photo:** The sun, the wind, and decades of quiet neglect have taken their toll on this former dry goods store.

NELSON STORY'S
CATTLE DRIVE

In 1858, Nelson Story, a 20-year-old adventurer from Ohio, headed west to make his fortune. He made his first $30,000 in a mining venture near Virginia City, then determined to invest part of it to accommodate beef-starved Montana miners. In 1866, Story purchased 600 Texas longhorns at $10 per head, hired 29 drovers, and armed them with Remington breechloaders.

Because of the opposition of Kansas farmers to longhorns and their "tick fever," Story blazed a new trail northwestward. Near Fort Reno, an Indian raiding party wounded two cowboys and drove off part of the herd, but Story promptly rode in pursuit, and his well-armed men scattered the warriors and recovered their cattle. Leaving his wounded men at the fort, Story proceeded up the Bozeman Trail, but he was stopped at Fort Phil Kearny by Colonel Henry Carrington, who had closed the trail because of hostile Indian activity.

One of the cowboys guarding the cattle near the fort was slain by lurking warriors, spurring Story's decision to defy the military and finish his drive. Pulling out after taps, Story and his men pushed up the trail all night to outdistance military pursuit.

The drive was so successful that Story decided to travel only at night, resting the herd during the day. As a result, there were only two more Indian attacks during the remainder of the journey. Each attack took place when the herd was under daytime guard, and the cowboys were able to drive the warriors away.

There was little danger past Fort Smith, and the daring drive was completed successfully. The $10 cattle were sold for $100 per head, Virginia City diners were assured of their beefsteaks, and Story was well on his way to achieving his dream of success.

After the Civil War, millions of longhorns were moved from Texas to Kansas. From there, some were shipped by rail to the Midwest, while others were driven northwest to become the foundation of present-day herds.

BANNACK

MONTANA

John White and several partners found gold along Montana's Grasshopper Creek on July 28, 1862. Soon, hundreds of Idaho prospectors hurried up the Mullan Road, a military highway, to get in on the strike. From a population of 400 in the fall of 1862, Bannack boomed to 800 the following spring, then to 3,000 by midsummer, with another 2,000 scattered around nearby diggings.

The notorious Henry Plummer was an early arrival in Bannack, and it wasn't long before he organized fellow criminals into a band of "Road Agents" or "Innocents" (the latter because one of their secret greetings was "I am innocent"). The Road Agents identified themselves by secret handshakes and neckerchief knots, and they were known to mark stagecoaches with code symbols indicating they were to be robbed.

A promontory three miles north of Bannack was the site of so many holdups that it was dubbed Road Agents' Rock. No one knows for certain how many solitary travelers and miners were killed at the

The road into the town of Bannack is a road into the past. No automobiles are allowed into this State Historic Park.

The building with the bell tower is the Masonic Lodge and school. The two-story structure in the center is the Montana Hotel, built in 1867. To the right of the hotel is a log residence that once served as a miners' rooming house and bar.

site for their possessions, but the total number of murders attributed to the Innocents across the region was calculated at 102.

Fugitive Jack Cleveland turned up in Bannack and threatened to reveal Plummer's secret leadership of the Innocents unless he received a cut of the action. On January 14, 1863, Plummer shot Cleveland to death in a gunfight in Goodrich's Saloon. The dying Cleveland whispered his information to blacksmith Hank Crawford, whose efforts to oppose the outlaw leader triggered another shootout. Plummer was wounded by a friend of Crawford's, but Hank wisely left town.

Impressed by Plummer's willingness to stand up to opponents—and unaware that he was ringleader of the Road Agents—the voters of Bannack elected him sheriff in May of 1863. Sheriff Plummer appointed two of his henchmen, Ned Ray and Buck Stinson, as deputies, and the following December he also became sheriff of Innocent-plagued Virginia City!

Plummer married young Electra Elizabeth O'Brien during June of 1863. Within less than three months, however, Mrs. Plummer went home to her parents, perhaps having learned of Henry's nefarious activities. Sheriff Plummer kept up

Dressed in their Sunday best, Bannack men idle away their free time on the porch of Fielding L. Graves' general store.

Top photo: The first successful bucket-lift dredge in the United States also was the first electric gold dredge in the world. Christened the "Fielding L. Graves" in 1895, the revolutionary machine attracted visitors from New York, Chicago, and abroad. One of the women in the rowboat is Mrs. H. J. Reiling, wife of the president of Gold Dredging Co.

Bottom photo: View of Bannack in 1900, looking west. Dredging took place in Grasshopper Creek, visible in the foreground.

appearances, however, providing a sumptuous feast for prominent citizens to celebrate Montana's first Thanksgiving.

A month later, Road Agent George Ives was hanged by vigilantes in Nevada City because he had murdered George Tiebalt for $200 in gold dust and a span of mules. A large vigilance committee of aroused citizens had been formed to counter the Road Agents, and the hanging of Ives triggered as many as 30 executions.

From two Road Agents hanged on January 4, 1864, the names of Henry Plummer, Buck Stinson, Ned Ray, and other Innocents were extracted. Six days later, the Bannack vigilante chapter seized

Below: 1895 photo of worker cleaning an electric dredge.

Plummer, Ray, and Stinson, hauling them to the gallows Plummer himself had requested for the hanging of a horse thief. Ray and Stinson died cursing, but Plummer begged for his life before swinging from the gallows.

With order firmly established, Bannack took shape along Main Street. When the Montana Territory was created in May of 1864, Bannack was named territorial capital. By the time the legislature convened in December, however, a new rush was on to Alder Gulch, and it was decided to move the capital to Virginia City. The legislature met in Bannack for two months, then transferred to Virginia City in February of 1865.

Bannack's citizenry was making the same move. The census of 1870 tallied just 762 residents, although the population remained at the same level for another decade. In 1875, Bannack became the seat of Beaverhead County, and a two-story brick courthouse was built for $14,000. After the county seat was moved to Dillon in 1882, the structure was remodeled into the Meade Hotel.

Eventually, Bannack shriveled to about 200 citizens, although there was a temporary increase around the turn of the century when five mining dredges clawed at the bed of Grasshopper Creek for a few years. The census of 1920 recorded just 59 residents, and by the 1940s Bannack was deserted.

Since then, Montana has turned Bannack into a state park, maintaining the old town as it was late in the 19th century. Automobile traffic is not permitted, and visitors may enjoy Bannack as a noncommercialized ghost town.

Left: Abandoned mine structures and piles of discarded tailings hint at the level of mining activity that occurred in Bannack as far back as a century ago. **Above:** This two-story building was erected as a courthouse in 1875. After the county seat was moved to Dillon in 1882, it was remodeled into the Meade Hotel. Purchased in 1931 by the I. B. Mining Company, the hotel was used as an office and a boarding house for miners until it was acquired by the state of Montana in 1954.

The lower floor of this building served as a school, while the upper floor was used as a Masonic Hall.

At one time, eight grades met in this schoolroom, but when the number of students finally exceeded capacity, grades six through eight were moved to the church, and a second teacher was assigned.

GAMBLER & SHOOTIST HENRY PLUMMER

Born in Maine in 1832, Henry Plummer received a solid education, then responded to the lure of the California gold fields. By the age of 19, he had opened a bakery with a partner in Nevada, and he supplemented his income by dealing faro.

Despite an affinity for saloons, gambling, and prostitutes, Plummer pinned on a badge as a Nevada City deputy. With the assistance of corrupt backers, Plummer soon became town marshal, but in 1857 he killed a man whose wife he was having an affair with, and he was sentenced to 10 years in San Quentin prison.

By 1859, Plummer had wrangled a pardon, along with reappointment as a Nevada City deputy. Two years later, he killed two men in separate bordello brawls. Arrested for murder again, Plummer bribed a jailer and escaped. Soon he turned up in Lewiston, Idaho, a booming mining town where he again worked as a faro dealer and began associating with desperadoes.

With the charisma of a born leader, Plummer courageously dispersed a Lewiston lynch mob, but in September of 1862, he and two confederates engaged in a wild shootout with dance hall owner Pat Ford. Plummer's horse and one of his friends were badly wounded, but Ford was shot dead, and most observers credited Henry with triggering the fatal round.

Plummer, then 30 years old, had enough sense to leave town in a hurry. The personable gambler and shootist would go on to achieve his true infamy in Bannack, Montana.

Bannack's graveyard, the final resting place for many of Henry Plummer's lynched Road Agents.

Top photo: Bannack's Methodist Church (second building from left) was built in 1877 under the direction of missionary William Van Orsdel. To the right of the church is a log dwelling that was sometimes used as a parsonage. The building at the far left is one of Montana's first frame residences, built in 1867 by carpenter William Roe and later acquired by prominent citizen Fielding L. Graves.

Bottom photo: No prisoner ever escaped from Bannack's small but sturdy jail, built in 1862 with eight inch (and larger) logs.

THE SOUTHWEST

TOMBSTONE
ARIZONA

Before veteran prospector Ed Schieffelin ventured alone into southern Arizona's San Pedro Valley, he was warned by a group of soldiers that he would find only his tombstone, as he would probably be killed by Apache warriors. Instead, he struck a fabulously wealthy silver vein, which he gleefully dubbed the Tombstone.

He also claimed the Graveyard, and on successive days he staked out the Toughnut and Lucky Cuss (so named because his brother said, "You lucky cuss!"). Other mines also were opened, and the first permanent house in Tombstone was built in April of 1879.

By 1880, Tombstone was the most famous mining town in the West, and the population soon soared to 15,000. Eastern capital poured in to develop the silver mines, and even though fires raged through the boomtown's business district in 1881 and 1882, Tombstone was rapidly rebuilt each time.

Tombstone's infamous Boot Hill. The nearby City Cemetery was reserved for "respectable" citizens.

Allen Street, Tombstone's main thoroughfare. In the foreground is the Crystal Palace Saloon, where Deputy U.S. Marshal Virgil Earp maintained a second-floor office. It was here, too, that the lawman was ambushed on the night of December 28, 1881, taking a shotgun blast in his left arm.

Allen Street was the main thoroughfare, although the ornate and imposing courthouse of newly organized (1882) Cochise County somehow ended up on Toughnut Street. Also built that year, on Fremont Street, was the similarly ornate City Hall, and looming nearby was the two-story Schieffelin Hall.

The *Tombstone Epitaph,* the town's newspaper, was assigned its picturesque label by founder John Clum, who pointed out that, "Every tombstone needs its epitaph." There were four churches, a two-story school with 250 students, an iron foundry, almost every type of store, and a bottling plant.

The bottles were clearly needed, because there were at least 110 establishments licensed to dispense liquor. The Crystal Palace, Oriental, and Hafford's Corner Saloon were among the most popular of Tombstone's watering holes. Rowdy entertainment was available around the clock at the Bird Cage Theatre, run by Joe Mignon and his wife, Big Minnie, a 230-pound blonde who often worked as the bouncer.

Prostitution in Tombstone was controlled by a Frenchman known as "The Count." The first madam he brought to Tombstone was Blonde Marie, who operated a house on Sixth Street and made enough money to return to France.

Other popular "soiled doves" of the time were Madam Moustache (Eleanor Dumont) and Crazy Horse Lil, the latter a robust woman who regularly became roaring drunk and looked for a fight with either women or men. Then there was Irish Mag, who displayed a classic heart of gold by grubstaking a customer who did not even pay for her services, but who struck it rich a few months later and repaid the investment with $500,000, allowing Mag to retire to Belfast, Ireland. But Tombstone's most famous mistress was Big Nose Kate Fisher, consort to gambler-gunfighter-dentist Doc Holliday.

Tombstone was a haven for men like Holliday. Gamblers flocked there, along with hordes of other shady characters, and when vast quantities of whiskey were thrown into the equation, it created an atmosphere of frequent violence. Such rampant lawlessness contributed to what became the West's most famous shootout, the gunfight at the O.K. Corral, which pitted five members of the Clanton-McLaury gang of stock thieves against the Earp brothers and Doc Holliday. Three of the rustlers were killed, and in the vicious aftermath,

The historic *Tombstone Epitaph* in its current offices on the west side of Fifth Street. First published in May of 1880, the newspaper provided extensive coverage of the now famous shootout pitting the Earp brothers and Doc Holliday against the Clantons and McLaurys.

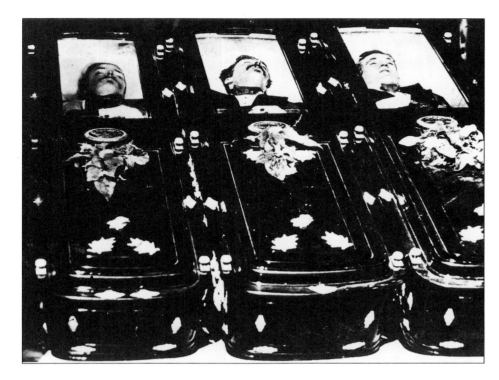

Top left: The bodies of Tom and Frank McLaury and Billy Clanton on display in the window of a hardware store. **Above:** (clockwise from top) Wyatt Earp (1848-1929), Virgil Earp (1843-1905), and Morgan Earp (1851-1882). A fourth brother, James (not pictured), was a saloonkeeper who had little to do with his brothers' activities. **Left:** At the 1937 Helldorado Festival, Tombstone residents erected a monument "To the Unknown Dead Too Slow on the Draw." Billy Breakenridge, a deputy sheriff during Tombstone's wild days, in 1928 published *Helldorado,* a book of reminiscences. The following year Tombstone, mired in severe decline, began an annual "Helldorado" celebration in an effort to spur tourism.

John Heath, mastermind of the "Bisbee Massacre," dangles from a telegraph pole on Toughnut Street. On December 8, 1883, five criminals fatally wounded four citizens (including a woman) during a holdup in Bisbee, a mining town south of Tombstone. When Heath tried to lead the pursuit party astray, he was arrested and soon confessed his complicity.

Morgan Earp and at least two more of the Clanton-McLaury contingent were gunned down in separate incidents.

The gunfight at the O.K. Corral assumed legendary proportions, but there was plenty of other action in Tombstone:

John Ringo shot Louis Hancock in the throat outside the Crystal Palace in December of 1879; three years later, Ringo was murdered and scalped in Turkey Creek Canyon east of Tombstone.

On June 22, 1880, a midnight shootout erupted outside the Cosmopolitan Hotel involving Buckskin Frank Leslie, who was having a conversation with May Killeen and her husband Mike; Frank was injured, but Mike was mortally wounded.

Tombstone's first city marshal, Fred White, was killed by Curly Bill Brocius on October 28, 1880.

Threatened by Billy Claiborne outside the Oriental Saloon on November 14, 1882, Buckskin Frank Leslie shot him to death.

On February 22, 1884, a lynch mob dragged John Heath out of the Tombstone jail and hanged him from a telegraph pole. Two weeks later, five of Heath's robbery accomplices were legally executed from a scaffold behind the courthouse.

Many of these and other victims were buried in Tombstone's famous Boot Hill, while more respectable citizens were laid to rest in the City Cemetery.

By the mid-1880s, the mine shafts were flooding. Slowly but surely the population declined, but many of the old buildings survived. Today, "the town too tough to die" is a popular destination for tourists.

Top photo: Tombstone after the fire of 1882. It was the second devastating blaze in as many years, but Tombstone rebuilt quickly both times. **Bottom photo:** Allen Street looking west from Fifth Street in 1929, the year the county seat was moved to Bisbee. The eight men in big hats at right are standing in front of the Crystal Palace Saloon.

A crowd surrounds the Modoc Stage, parked in front of the transportation company's first-floor office on the north side of Fremont Street, in 1888. On the second floor was the first courtroom of Cochise County. Next door (left) was the original office of the *Tombstone Epitaph,* which by 1888 had merged with the *Tombstone Prospector.* To the immediate right of the stage office was the Oriental Saloon, where Doc Holliday dealt cards and maintained a second-floor office (marked by an "x"). **Opposite page:** The Crystal Palace Saloon in 1882. Opened in 1879 as the Golden Eagle Brewery, the bar and gambling house was renamed after a customer exclaimed that the mirrors and chandeliers made the room look like a crystal palace.

GUNFIGHT AT THE
O.K. CORRAL

Top photo: Tombstone's "Wild Bunch" stages entertaining and historically accurate reenactments of the gunfight at the O. K. Corral.
Above: Entrance to the O. K. Corral on the north side of Allen Street. The famous shootout took place at the rear of the block-long establishment, on Fremont Street.

Just outside Tombstone's O.K. Corral, on the afternoon of October 26, 1881, a brief but furious exchange of gunfire between eight men became the most celebrated shootout in the history of the Old West.

For months, ill feelings had festered between the two warring factions, the Clanton-McLaury ring of rustlers, and the Earp brothers, who represented the law in various capacities (although rumor held that the Earps and their ally, Doc Holliday, were surreptitiously involved in criminal activities as well).

Following several incidents in Tombstone that nearly resulted in violence between the two groups, City Marshal Virgil Earp, accompanied by "deputies" Wyatt and Morgan Earp and Doc Holliday, marched to the O.K. Corral to confront Ike and Billy Clanton and Frank and Tom McLaury.

"Throw up your hands!" shouted Virgil, and the shooting started. Ike dashed for safety, while 18-year-old Billy Clanton and the McLaury brothers were fatally wounded. Morgan and Virgil also were hit, in the shoulder and leg, respectively, and Doc Holliday was grazed in the hip.

Doc and the Earps recovered from their wounds, but the war was not over. In retribution, Virgil was ambushed two months later, sustaining a shotgun blast that permanently crippled his left arm. Three months after that, Morgan was assassinated while playing a game of billiards. Wyatt and Doc participated in at least two vengeance killings before moving on to New Mexico.

Opposite page: The Lucky Cuss Saloon was named after a mine discovered by Ed Schieffelin. According to local legend, the prospector chose the name for his mine after his brother Al had exclaimed, "You lucky cuss!"

Top photo: General store from Tombstone's early days. **Middle:** Contemporary cowboys pose in front of one of the many specialty stores catering to tourists. **Bottom:** A jewelry store occupies the building that once housed the Oriental Saloon, built by Milt Joyce in 1880 at the corner of Allen and Fifth. Luke Short killed fellow gambler Charles Storms inside the Oriental in 1881, and the next year Buckskin Frank Leslie fatally wounded Billy the Kid Claiborne on the sidewalk at left.

THE LEGENDARY
BIRD CAGE THEATRE

The Bird Cage Theatre opened in Tombstone on December 23, 1881, and its doors did not close for nine years. Located on Allen Street at Sixth, the Bird Cage was an immediate sensation, dispensing whiskey, women, gambling, and other forms of entertainment 24 hours a day, often to standing-room-only crowds.

A trio of red-coated bartenders worked the bar, which featured a dumbwaiter used to send liquor upstairs. Behind the bar was a nine-foot-tall painting of Fatima, a popular belly dancer of that era, that became scarred through the years with the accumulation of six bullet holes. The walls and ceilings acquired no less than 140 bullet holes, the result of at least 16 gunfights and a lot of overly exuberant customers.

Two bits to the doorman was the cost of admission to the main room, flanked by six balcony alcoves on either side. Each alcove and the girl inside could be hired for $25, giving birth to the familiar refrain about a "bird in a gilded cage."

The orchestra pit boasted a massive grand piano, and the burlesque shows sometimes yielded to Lotta Crabtree, Eddie Foy, and other national headliners who were brave enough to face frontier audiences. When *Uncle Tom's Cabin* was performed on the Bird Cage stage in June 1882, a drunken cowboy in the audience shot the bloodhound that was supposed to be chasing the character Eliza!

Below the stage were a wine cellar, dressing rooms, and a poker table where seats went for $1,000 in chips. This house game may well have been the longest-running in Western history; play continued nonstop for eight years, five months, and three days.

The Bird Cage Theatre opened in 1881 and operated nonstop for nine raucous years. A considerable number of Tombstone's "respectable" citizens would not enter the Bird Cage, prompting many acts to stage additional performances in Schieffelin Hall before leaving town.

SILVERBELL
ARIZONA

They called it "the hellhole of Arizona." The harsh description seems to have accurately labeled Silverbell, a remote copper-mining town, at the turn of the century. There was a level of outlawry comparable to other isolated communities of this raw territory, and more than the usual number of gunfights, knifings, and murders. One local doctor is said to have kept a large tomato can on his desk that was half full of bullets removed from Silverbell shooting victims.

A particularly bloody shootout erupted on Monday night, October 2, 1905, when four cowboys left Webster's Saloon. As they walked down the street they passed three Mexicans, one of whom, apparently drunk, was being supported by his two companions. Suddenly, without evident provocation, the Mexicans drew their weapons and opened fire at the backs of the Anglos.

Three of the men were wounded, two fatally, while the

Mine ruins near Silverbell. High-grade copper deposits were discovered in the Silver Bell Mountains during the 1860s.

By the 1920s, mining production had almost ceased. Silverbell deteriorated rapidly; within a few years, the one-time "hellhole of Arizona" was abandoned.

The Imperial Copper Company extended the Arizona Southern Railroad from Red Rock to Silverbell, a distance of 20 miles, in 1904, beginning the rowdiest period of the old mining camp.

murderers fled on foot. There was a massive manhunt throughout the countryside, but the two primary suspects had hidden in town. They were apprehended on October 6, when they tried to catch a train.

Although the Arizona Rangers never had more than 26 men on their roster, one was never far from Silverbell. Private Reuben Burnett was stationed in Silverbell in 1905, and later that same year he was replaced by Private Henry McPhaul. Eventually, Pima County assigned Deputy Sheriff Sam McEven to the town. Known as a no-nonsense peace officer, McEven systematically curbed lawlessness, arresting lawbreakers and rigorously enforcing a local ordinance against carrying firearms.

When Ramon Castro killed Gracio Manzo, Castro hid in an old mine tunnel for two weeks. After McEven located Castro's hideout, he resourcefully hung a lantern from an ore car, then shoved the movable shield ahead of him until he had cornered the fugitive. Within a few months, the Ranger had tamed the proverbial hellhole.

Prospectors discovered high-grade copper in the Silver Bell Mountains in the 1860s. Companies soon moved in, bought the most promising

claims, and developed a number of mines. The mining camp of Silverbell flourished until the early 1880s, when low prices caused abandonment of the townsite.

Within two decades, however, the Imperial Copper Company was organized to reopen the Silverbell deposits in response to the enormous demand for copper telephone wiring. The company purchased the Old Boot and Mammoth mines and resumed operations, resurrecting the old camp.

The Arizona Southern Railroad extended a line from Red Rock in 1904, the same year the Silver-

bell post office was established. The population grew to 3,000 as annual production routinely exceeded $1 million. The Southern Arizona Smelting Company erected a major smelter nearby, and in 1917 Silverbell copper production peaked at a value of more than $2.1 million.

But the owners suffered losses at other mines, staggering the subsidiary Imperial Copper Company. To complicate matters, there was a shaft fire in Silverbell in 1911. A new company took over, but sagging copper prices halted production in 1921, and in 1934 the railroad tracks were torn up. Soon the entire population had departed, and today, only a cemetery remains at the Silverbell town site.

In 1951, however, a new Silver Bell (two words, this time) arose four miles to the southeast of the one-time hellhole. The American Smelting and Refining Company reopened an open-pit copper mine, and Silver Bell was built as a company town for 225 families.

Production eventually dwindled until, in the 1980s, Silver Bell was dismantled, and most of the buildings were moved to private property throughout the valley. Perhaps some day yet another Silverbell will be born in the historic old mountains.

Spread photo: A lonely cemetery is all that remains of Silverbell today. **Right:** A cradle grave—wire mesh shaped like a cradle with a cross on top. **Inset photo:** A more traditional headstone marks the grave of this former Silverbell resident.

MARY ANN O'TOOLE
APR 28, 1867
JAN 16, 1930
The hour of my departure comes,
I hear the voice that calls me home.
The race appointed I have run.
The combat's over, the prize is won.

Right: A huge demand for copper telephone wiring kept Silverbell alive after the turn of the century. **Below:** Miners assemble with their pack animals on the outskirts of town. **Bottom right:** Old mining equipment still litters the area around Silverbell.

A COMPANY TOWN
SASCO

An acronym for the Southern Arizona Smelting Company, Sasco was a company town built 13 miles northeast of Silverbell in 1907.

There was an enormous smelter at Sasco that was used to process ore from the Silverbell mines and the Picacho Mining Company. The Southern Arizona Smelting Company employed 175 men, and Sasco boasted a population of more than 600.

The biggest building in town was the stone Rockland Hotel, but the two-story city hall also was impressive, and there were numerous other masonry structures.

During Sasco's decline, which was already evident in 1919, a man named Charley Coleman rode the train up from Bisbee to confront his wife, who rented a room in a saloon and consorted with a number of men. Coleman barged into her room, threatened to kill two of her swains, and argued loudly with her—until the saloon owner killed him with a rifle bullet.

Also killed in 1919 were several Sasco citizens who succumbed to the influenza epidemic that dispatched half a million Americans across the country.

Sasco itself was dying because of the closure of the smelter, which had become unprofitable. The post office shut down on September 15, 1921, and Sasco was soon deserted. Today, ghost town hunters can explore the remains of the Rockland Hotel, Sasco City Hall, the depot, and other buildings.

SHAKESPEARE
NEW MEXICO

Mexican Springs, the eventual site of Shakespeare, was used as a watering hole for travelers in the 1850s and as a stop for the Butterfield Stage's southern route in 1858.

Abandoned during the Civil War, the stage stop was rebuilt by the National Mail and Transportation Company in 1867 and renamed Grant in honor of the most famous Union hero of the war. The new station keeper was "Uncle Johnny" Evenson, who cooked antelope steaks and biscuits for wayfarers until 1888.

In 1872, W. D. Brown, a member of a government survey party, recognized silver in the nearby Pyramid Mountains and hurried with ore samples to San Francisco, where he interested financier William Ralston. Having already made a fortune from the Comstock Lode around Virginia City, Nevada, Ralston sent Brown with an expedition to establish claims in the

For more than two decades, Uncle Johnny Evenson cooked antelope steaks for patrons of the Grant House.

View of Shakespeare today, with Avon Avenue running left to right across the page. The Grant House is visible at left. Across the street at the far left is what used to be the town's general store.

"Virginia Mining District." The district would center on the stage station, and the booming mining camp was christened Ralston. As many as 3,000 prospectors swarmed into the Pyramid Mountains, but most of the ore proved to be low-grade, necessitating mining machinery to work the claims profitably. Ralston, however, had not filed according to New Mexico laws, and the boom soon ended as the prospectors tried their luck elsewhere.

Colonel John Boyle of St. Louis stepped into the picture in 1877 as a representative of the Shakespeare Mining Company, a name inspired by its large number of British investors. Eventually, the mining town took the bard's name as well. The most productive mines were the 85, Atwood, Henry Clay, and Yellow Jacket. The population of Shakespeare stabilized at about 300, mostly miners and their families.

Avon Avenue, Shakespeare's aptly named main street, was lined with solid adobe buildings.

There were two hostelries, the Grant House and the Stratford Hotel.

The finest of the three or four saloons was the Roxy Jay, which boasted a polished mahogany bar that ran the entire length of the building and an enormous mirror shipped overland from St. Louis. Poverty Flat, the red-light district, was just northwest of town.

In 1881, a "substantial calaboose" was erected in Shakespeare. First to occupy the new jail were rustlers Sandy King and Russian Bill, but a vigilante group voted to lynch the desperadoes, leaving them hanging from a rafter of the dining room of the Grant House as an example to potential troublemakers. When the stagecoach unloaded passengers the next morning for breakfast, they were greeted by the dangling corpses. The passengers buried the victims in a common grave at the western edge of Shakespeare Cemetery, and one of the impromptu morticians took Russian Bill's fine boots as a fee.

Shakespeare's Avon Avenue in the early 1880s, when the population reached 300. The town was big enough to offer several stores and saloons, plus two hotels. The stage road intersected Avon Avenue from the left.

As mine production lagged, the population departed, and Shakespeare lost its post office in 1885. Most of the buildings were deserted by the 1890s, but in 1907 the Atwood, 85, and Henry Clay mines were reopened. The Stratford Hotel also reopened, providing lodging for miners. The Southern Pacific ran a spur line down Avon Avenue to the new mining village of Valedon, two miles to the south.

The mines finally closed during the Depression, and in 1935 Frank Hill acquired the town site as part of his ranch. Frank, his wife, and later his daughter Janaloo worked persistently to maintain the surviving structures. Today the Grant House, Stratford Hotel, general store, and a few other buildings remain intact, and for years Janaloo has staged performances for tourists.

Above: Chief Victorio of the Eastern Chiricahua Apaches. Born around 1825 in southwestern New Mexico—the area in which Shakespeare later would take shape—Victorio became a superb guerrilla fighter. Reluctantly submitting to reservation life, Victorio repeatedly led breakouts, raiding in New Mexico, Arizona, and Mexico. The ferocious chief was slain during an 1880 ambush in Mexico in which most of his followers were killed or captured. **Left:** The O. R. Smyth residence was built in Shakespeare in 1881, but only the foundation remains today.

The Grant House offered travelers a dining room and overnight accommodations. Windows in the adobe structure were much larger than was considered safe during the long years of warfare against Apaches, but rocks were piled against the inside walls so the building could be quickly fortified if necessary.

WALDEMAR TETHENBORN
RUSSIAN BILL

Waldemar Tethenborn was born around 1850 in a Russian seaport on the Baltic Sea. His father was a Russian subject, but his mother was the daughter of Scottish sea captain William Rogers. A cavalryman in Russia's Imperial Army until some scandal (possibly involving a duel with a superior officer) forced him to flee the country, Waldemar went to sea and altered his name to William Rogers Tethenborn, but he was nicknamed "Russian Bill."

Debarking at San Francisco, Russian Bill drifted through the West in search of adventure. A dashing figure with shoulder-length blond hair, fancy hand-tooled boots, and a penchant for reciting poetry when he was drunk, he was lamed in a Fort Worth shootout, slashed in the shoulder in a Denver knife fight, then, along with rustler Sandy King, sur-

vived a hard-fought battle with Arizona ranchers early in November 1881. Soon afterward, Bill and King were arrested at Deming, New Mexico, and jailed at Shakespeare.

At 2 a.m. on November 9, 1881, a mob seized the two prisoners and hanged them from a rafter of the Grant House. King was executed because he was a longtime outlaw, Russian Bill because he had stolen a horse, though several different accounts of the incident suggest he may have been unfairly accused of the crime.

A Silver City newspaper reported that, in response to a query from a U. S. consul in Russia on behalf of a "lady of quality" concerned about her son, Sheriff Harvey Whitehill tactfully replied that Russian Bill had passed away "from a shortage of breath due to a sudden change in altitude."

The noose dangling from the ceiling of the Grant House is a macabre reminder of the night in 1881 when Russian Bill and Sandy King were taken from Shakespeare's jail and lynched here from one of the rafters.

Opposite page: The rear of the Grant House (inset) was sometimes used as a bar. **Above:** Shakespeare Cemetery. Lynched outlaws Russian Bill and Sandy King were dumped into a common grave on the western edge of Shakespeare's "bone orchard."

WHITE OAKS
NEW MEXICO

It took three decades for John J. Barnett to strike paydirt, but the frustrated forty-niner finally located the gold lode that gave birth to the town of White Oaks in Lincoln County, New Mexico.

Barnett took in two other prospectors, John Winters and John H. Wilson, to help him work the strike. Soon, Barnett and Winters bought out Wilson for about $40 in gold washings, two dollars in silver coins, and a revolver. The two remaining partners later sold out for $300,000 each, and eventually, $4.5 million worth of bullion was mined from Baxter's original discovery area.

At first, clusters of tents were scattered throughout the mountainous region. These hastily assembled mini-communities included Tent Town, Shanty Town, Hide Town, Boot Hill, and Hogtown, the latter comprised of brothels, saloons, and gambling dens. When White Oaks, named after a nearby spring,

The two-story brick school, built in 1894 for $10,000, still dominates the north side of town.

White Oaks Saloon. The era of wide-open saloons, gambling dens, and brothels was over by the mid-1880s, as solid citizens began to dominate town life.

began to take shape, it was just as wild as other mining camps.

Late in 1880, for example, Billy the Kid and fellow desperadoes Dave Rudabaugh and Billy Wilson rode down White Oaks Avenue and threw a wild shot at a deputy sheriff. Cornered by a posse at the ranch of Jim Greathouse, the fugitives killed Deputy Sheriff Jim Carlyle and escaped into the darkness, while the lawmen angrily burned the ranch house to the ground.

In 1882, a horse thief was taken from his "cell" (a 30-foot dry well in the middle of White Oaks) and hanged. But this was White Oaks' only lynching, because by this point, community leadership was becoming dominated by mine owners and managers, men from the East with education and breeding who intended to make the town suitable for their families.

"The town never had a red-light district, or any noticeable number of wild women," reminisced Morris Parker, son of one of the leading families. "The early-day boomtown atmosphere, featuring saloons, wide-open gambling, and guns and Bowie knives dangling from belts, had practically disappeared [by 1885]."

White Oaks Avenue, 100 feet wide and half a mile long, was the main street. There were boardwalks in front of the buildings, the most impressive of which was the Exchange Bank. The principal hotel was the two-story Ozanne. There was also an opera house, and in 1894 a two-story brick school was built that still dominates the north end of town. A big town hall became the center of all public activities, including church services.

White Oaks never developed any public utilities, and until 1901 the nearest telegraph line was at Fort Stanton, more than 20 miles to the south. Water from the town's wells was hard and brackish, so a water wagon filled 40-gallon barrels for 50 cents.

White Oaks is believed to have the deepest gold mines in the United States and possibly the world. There were nine substantial mines in the vicinity, the most important of which were the Old Abe (the leader at 1,350 feet), the North Homestake (800 feet), and the South Homestake (1,066 feet). In 1893, an exploding kerosene lamp caused a horrible shaft fire in the Old Abe, killing nine miners, and mine production soon began to sag.

When the El Paso and Northeastern Railroad began laying tracks in the area shortly after the turn of the century, White Oaks' city fathers tried to charge exorbitant amounts of money for rights-of-way. As a result, the railroad was routed several miles to the west, and White Oaks, which had boasted a lively population of 2,500 in the 1890s, began its rapid decline into a picturesque ghost.

Miners toiling in the Old Abe Mine in September of 1898. Five years earlier, nine miners were killed by a shaft fire in the Old Abe, but the mine eventually produced $3 million worth of gold.

The first mine on Baxter Mountain was the North Homestake, but soon there was the South Homestake, Old Abe, Comstock, Rip Van Winkle, Little Mack, Queen of God, Smuggler, Captain Kidd, Black Prince, Little Nell, Large Hopes, Forty-Four, Discovery, Hoosier Boy—and, shown here, the Henry Clay.

Top photo: The Exchange Bank was built on the north side of White Oaks Avenue. Attorney John Y. Hewitt, whose offices were upstairs, was president of the bank and editor of the *White Oaks Eagle*.
Bottom: Today, several ranch families continue to occupy homes around the old townsite.

WATSON HOYLE'S IMPRESSIVE FOLLY

In 1892, Watson Hoyle, superintendent and part owner of White Oaks' richest mine, the Old Abe, built a beautiful Victorian mansion on the southeast corner of Lincoln Avenue and Grand Street.

The two-story "Hoyle Castle" was the most impressive residence in town, boasting hand-carved pine-and-redwood paneling, stained-glass windows, and a lead-pipe water system. Its total cost was estimated to be well over $60,000.

But the interior of this grand house was never finished, and Hoyle never completely furnished it. Hoyle was a bachelor, and it was rumored that he was very much in love, but that his bride-to-be either rejected the mine owner and returned to her Eastern home, or that she married a simple cowboy instead.

Whether or not these rumors were true, Hoyle lived for years in his uncompleted mansion with only his brother and sister-in-law for company. By the time Watt Hoyle moved elsewhere, his splendid home had been dubbed "Hoyle's Folly."

By 1885 there were more than 200 houses in White Oaks, but the town's finest residence was the two-story brick "Hoyle Castle," built in 1892 by Watson Hoyle, manager and part owner of the Old Abe Mine.

LINCOLN
NEW MEXICO

Mexican-American settlers in the 1850s established a pioneer community they named La Placita del Rio Bonito ("The Little Town by the Pretty River"). They erected a round stone *torreon* (tower) as a refuge from attack by Apache raiders, and additional protection was available from Fort Stanton, established 10 miles to the west in 1855.

As the town developed, flat-roofed adobes were built on either side of the only street, which ran roughly a mile east to west, parallel to the Rio Bonito.

A reenactment of a Western shootout staged during Billy the Kid Days.

The community was called "Rio Bonito" or "La Placita" until 1869, when it was renamed Lincoln and made the county seat. Lincoln County covered 27,000 square miles and was the largest county in the United States. Comprising the entire southeastern quarter of loosely governed New Mexico, Lincoln County was inadequately policed by a sheriff and a handful of deputies, making frontier outlawry and violence almost inevitable.

The adobe buildings of Lincoln date from the town's violent frontier days during the 1870s and 1880s.

View of Lincoln in 1886. The two-story structure (seen from the rear) in the middle of the photo is "The Big House." The long building across the street and to the left is the Wortley Hotel. Lincoln's only street ambles to the right, roughly paralleling the Rio Bonito, indicated by the tree line just above town.

The Horrell War involved five quarrelsome brothers from Texas (a sixth brother had already been slain in a Las Cruces shootout), who were known rustlers and killers and who re-established their family near Lincoln. Soon there was a bloody gunfight in Lincoln, and one of the four victims was the youngest Horrell brother.

Vowing revenge, the surviving Horrells raided a wedding dance in Lincoln in December of 1873, killing four men and wounding two others. The Horrells were driven back to Texas (where three more of the brothers were killed during the next few years) by a group of local vigilantes.

Such violence created an atmosphere in which the notorious Lincoln County War would thrive. Lawrence G. Murphy built a mercantile business in Lincoln, which was headquartered at the town's largest building, dubbed "The Big House." Murphy's empire soon expanded by shady methods to include land and cattle, and Sheriff William Brady was a willing associate.

Eventually, cattle baron John Chisum came into conflict with Murphy, and he exacerbated the clash by establishing lawyer Alexander McSween in a competing store in Lincoln. A young rancher from England, John Tunstall, invested in the enterprise, and a bank was formed: Chisum was the president, Tunstall the vice-president, and Mc-Sween the secretary-treasurer.

At this point, Lincoln boasted at least 500 residents. The only hostelry was the Wortley Hotel, across from the Big House. The latter dominated the west end of town, while the large Chisum-Tunstall-McSween store was in the middle of Lincoln, just west of the *torreon* and on the north side of the road. McSween's sprawling adobe house was next door to the store. The McSweens owned the only piano in town, and their house was the social center of Lincoln—until full-scale war erupted.

Sheriff Brady and a large posse murdered John Tunstall south of Lincoln on February 18, 1878. Billy the Kid and other "Regulators" rode in vengeance, killing Brady and a deputy on Lincoln's main street on April 1. The Lincoln County War escalated in violence for five months, then came to a head in mid-July in one of the greatest gunfights in Western history.

On the night of July 14, nearly 50 Regulators slipped into Lincoln, while an almost equal number of their adversaries slept in and around the Big House. Billy the Kid and 13 other gunmen barricaded themselves inside Alexander McSween's U-shaped, 12-room adobe house, while other Regulators were stationed in surrounding buildings. At dawn, the Regulators opened fire on their startled foes, beginning two days of sniping.

On the third day the Regulators severely wounded a deputy, and on the fourth day the commander of nearby Fort Stanton sent out a large detail of troops with a howitzer and a Gatling gun. The military camped in the east end

From top to bottom: Cattle baron John Chisum clashed with Lawrence Murphy and his Big House faction; attorney Alexander McSween operated the Chisum-Tunstall store in Lincoln and was killed during the Battle of Lincoln; Englishman John Henry Tunstall, who hired Billy the Kid and whose murder triggered the Lincoln County War.

of town and declared their neutrality, but their imposing presence intimidated the McSween men. By the fifth day, July 19, most of the McSween force had slipped across the Rio Bonito, vanishing into the rugged countryside.

McSween's adobe was set afire, and by that night the slow blaze had consumed all but four rooms. After dark the defenders came out shooting. There were casualties on both sides, but McSween was among the dead, and his surviving supporters became outlaws. Billy the Kid was captured, shot his way out of incarceration in the Big House, then was tracked down and killed by Sheriff Pat Garrett.

In 1913, with the wild days long past and Lincoln reduced to a backwater, the county seat was moved to Carrizozo. Lincoln's population dipped to about 50, but the Big House remained, and so did the other store, the *torreon,* and almost all of the other buildings. Today's visitor can stay at the Wortley Hotel and tour one of the West's least changed historic towns.

Whelan & Co., a mercantile business that operated on the north side of Lincoln's main street from 1886 through 1890.

The Tunstall-McSween store, located in the middle of the north side of Lincoln's main street, continued to operate under other owners for decades after the Lincoln County War. The interior is shown here in 1954; today the historic building is operated as a museum.

When Lincoln was settled during the 1850s, there was constant danger of Indian attack, so this stone *torreon* was built in the middle of town as a defensive strongpoint. During the Battle of Lincoln, gunfighters manned the old tower.

Top photo: Sam Wortley built a small hotel across the street from the Big House at the west end of town. When the Big House was converted into the county courthouse and jail, prisoners were fed at the Wortley Hotel, which still offered accommodations to travelers. **Bottom:** One of many historical buildings in Lincoln is the former house and office of Dr. Woods.

Left: The most famous photo of Billy the Kid was first printed in reverse, erroneously indicating that he was a left-handed gun. **Top of page:** Ad announcing a reward for Billy the Kid issued by Governor Lew Wallace, who spent most of his time in Santa Fe writing *Ben-Hur.* **Above:** Sheriff Pat Garrett, who ended the life of Billy the Kid.

WESTERN LEGEND
BILLY THE KID

William Bonny, alias Billy the Kid, became a Western legend during New Mexico's bloody Lincoln County War.

While still a teenager, he fatally wounded a blacksmith in a saloon near Camp Grant, Arizona, then fled to lawless Lincoln County. The Kid was hired by English rancher John Tunstall, who was feuding with a faction centered in Lincoln and who was himself brutally murdered on February 18, 1878. Lusting for revenge, the Kid joined a band of "Regulators" who hatched a plan that dispatched two of the suspected murderers.

On April 1, the Kid boldly set an ambush in Lincoln, leading four other Regulators to a low adobe wall overlooking the main thoroughfare. The five concealed gunmen killed Sheriff William Brady, who was the ringleader of Tunstall's murder, along with one of his deputies.

After this spectacular coup there was an all-out war, climaxing in a five-day battle. The Kid shot his way to safety, but soon yielded to custody in expectation of amnesty from Territorial Governor Lew Wallace. But the Kid became apprehensive and escaped, rustling horses and engaging in several shootouts until his capture by Sheriff Pat Garrett in December of 1880.

Sentenced to hang, the Kid was incarcerated in Lincoln, but on May 13, 1881, he got hold of a gun and killed guards J. W. Bell and Bob Olinger, then made a leisurely escape past a passive citizenry.

The relentless Garrett renewed his pursuit and finally shot his prey to death in Fort Sumner on July 14, 1881.

Woodcut depicting the killing of Billy the Kid (holding knife). Concerned about the late-night arrival of strangers at the ranch compound where he was living, the Kid slipped into the rancher's home to find out who they were. Pat Garrett was waiting for him.

Lincoln County remains ranching country, and longhorn cattle still graze on ranges near Lincoln.

LINCOLN COUNTY'S
BIG HOUSE

In 1874, Lawrence G. Murphy built a large two-story structure on the west edge of Lincoln, just south of the road, as the headquarters of his commercial enterprise. "The Big House" contained a general store on the ground floor, as well as a billiard room, office, post office, storeroom, and bunkroom.

The second floor contained four bedrooms and another storeroom. Located behind the building were a cookhouse, privy, and several corrals.

Murphy was plunged into bankruptcy during the Lincoln County War, and local government officials purchased the building for a courthouse. Sheriff Pat Garrett built outside stairs in front and utilized the upstairs rooms for his office, the guardroom, an armory, and a jail.

The jail's most famous prisoner, Billy the Kid, pro-

cured a revolver (probably on a visit to the privy), killed two guards, and made a sensational escape on May 13, 1881.

During the mid-1880s, upstairs partitions were removed to provide a courtroom. When the county seat was moved to Carri-

zozo in 1913, the old courthouse was used as a community center and, for a time, as a school. In 1937, the State of New Mexico took over the building, and for decades now this historic old landmark has captivated tourists and Western history buffs alike.

The Big House dominated the west end of Lincoln. After the store became the Lincoln County courthouse, Billy the Kid was incarcerated in the front upstairs corner room at left.

VIRGINIA CITY
NEVADA

"Money was plenty as dust; every individual considered himself wealthy, and a melancholy countenance was nowhere to be seen," observed an enthusiastic, young Mark Twain after arriving in Virginia City, Nevada, in 1863.

"There were military companies, fire companies, brass bands, banks, hotels, theaters, hurdy-gurdy houses, wide-open gambling palaces, political powwows, civic processions, street fights, murders, inquests, riots, a whiskey mill every fifteen steps, a dozen breweries, and half a dozen jails and station houses in full operation, and some talk of building a church."

Actually, there were four churches—and more than 100 saloons. Virginia City sat atop the Comstock Lode, the richest silver deposit in the world, and during its

Virginia City today, looking northwest. St. Mary's in the Mountains is in the center of the photo, and St. Paul's Episcopal Church is just to the right of it.

Virginia City's main thoroughfare always has been C Street, which today remains busy with tourists. At left is the Red Garter Saloon Museum.

Looking north on C Street late in the 19th century. Nevada's first skyscraper, the six-story International Hotel, is just right of center. The magnificent hotel was built in 1877 for $200,000, with another $50,000 thrown in for furnishings and the first elevator in the West. The hotel burned in 1912.

boisterous heyday the "Queen of the Comstock" was the world's wealthiest city. More than $400 million in bullion was mined from the depths of the California, Belcher, Gould & Curry, Ophir, and other mines that honeycombed the rock beneath Virginia City.

Forty-niners had found gold traces in Gold Canyon and Six-Mile Canyon, adjacent to what would be named Mt. Davidson, but pressed on to California for more promising claims. By 1859, however, prospectors were panning profitably at a ramshackle camp they called Gold Hill.

At the north end of Six-Mile Canyon, deposits were found that contained more silver than gold. Ore from the Comstock Lode (named after loud-mouthed mine owner Henry Comstock) likewise contained impressive amounts of gold and silver. Mining companies quickly moved in, and dozens of large-scale operations introduced industrialization—and pollution—to the area.

James Fennimore, a prospector from Virginia known as "Old Virginny Finney," drunkenly dropped his whiskey bottle, and as he watched the precious liquor ooze across the rocks, he

Left: Reenactment in 1933 of an ore car being hauled to the elevator of the Consolidated Virginia Mine. **Below:** A sign overlooking Gold Canyon explains the significance of the site, which ultimately produced even more silver than gold. **Bottom of page:** Abandoned mine at Gold Canyon.

... THIS IS ...
GOLD CANYON

Gold Was Discovered at the Mouth of this Canyon Dayton, Nev., in 1849. Yet it took Ten Years for Prospectors To Work Their Way Up the Canyon to Uncover the Fabulous Silver Lode at Virginia City. By 1863 this Ravine, From Dayton to Virginia, A Distance of Seven Miles, Was A Continuous City of Mines, Mills, Stores, Homes, Restaurants, Offices, Saloons and Fandango Houses. An Endless Stream of Traffic Passed Here Headed *for* Virginia City. For A Fine Souvenir of Virginia City Get Your Copy of the Territorial Enterprise, Nevada's First Newspaper - *Home of Mark Twain Museum*

sadly pronounced, "I christen this ground Virginia." Thus named, Virginia City quickly reached boomtown proportions.

The first thoroughfare, A Street, was laid out north and south part of the way up the east side of 7,900-foot Mt. Davidson. Within a year there were several thousand inhabitants and hundreds of buildings.

Built on the side of a mountain, Virginia City "had a slant to it like a roof," according to Mark Twain. B Street was on the slope below A Street; C Street, still further down the slope, became the main thoroughfare; and D Street, just below, was the home of hundreds of prostitutes.

The town plat went all the way down to P Street, although the lower streets were never developed. The Victorian mansions of wealthy mine owners and merchants were perched above A Street, on Howard and Stewart Streets. When precipitous cross streets were formed, frequent wagon wrecks and runaways occurred, especially during icy winter months.

By 1864, narrow business lots in choice locations were selling for as much as $20,000. More than 25,000 people bustled through the streets of Virginia City and adjoining Gold Hill. Two-story brick commercial buildings abounded by 1865, along with imposing residences, fine churches and schools, two theatres, and three daily newspapers.

On October 26, 1875, fire broke out in a rooming house and destroyed 33 blocks, but Virginia City was rebuilt even more lavishly than before. The most impressive structures were the Storey County Courthouse, Piper's Opera House, St. Mary's in the Mountains Catholic Church, and the six-story International Hotel.

Surrounding the community were enormous mine and mill buildings, and as the years passed, the barren landscape began to be dotted by huge mounds of tailings. Indeed, beneath Virginia City was an "underground city" with about 30 miles of tunnels and drifts; the Gould & Curry Mine, for example, employed 500 miners to work five miles of tunnel.

Underground conditions were extremely hot (130 degrees Fahrenheit in some shafts) and dangerous, causing miners to unionize and secure an 8-hour workday and above-average wages. As many as 10,000 miners worked the Comstock Lode. It is estimated that more than 300 were killed in accidents, while another 600 were maimed or crippled.

The biggest year was 1876, when $38.5 million worth of bullion was hoisted out of the mines. The ensuing decline in production accompanied a drop in silver prices, caused largely by government policies that began in 1878.

By the turn of the century, Virginia City was a mere shadow of its early days, and by mid-century the population stood at less than 500. But many of the grand old structures still stand, and from May through October, C Street teems with tourists.

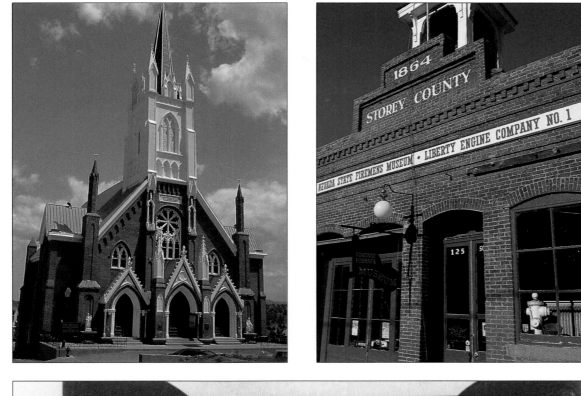

Far left: St. Mary's in the Mountains. The Catholic priest and nuns assigned here cared for Virginia City's poor and needy. After the fire of 1875, the church was magnificently rebuilt with generous donations from wealthy citizens. **Left:** The Nevada State Fireman's Museum is appropriately housed in an 1864 firehouse. **Below left and right:** Piper's Opera House on B Street faced the rear of the International Hotel.

Above: In 1862, unsuccessful prospector Samuel Clemens began working as a reporter for Virginia City's *Territorial Enterprise,* soon adopting the pen name Mark Twain. **Right:** The Silver Queen Saloon boasts one of the tallest bars in the world, elegant French mirrors—and the Silver Queen herself; the artwork is 15 feet tall and adorned with more than 3,000 silver dollars.

"SOILED DOVE"
JULIA BULETTE

Julia Bulette was a dark-eyed Creole from New Orleans who turned up when Virginia City was only a year old, a raw boomtown of tents and flimsy structures. Evidently, she was very successful plying her trade as a prostitute on Rampart Street, eventually setting up an elegant parlor house.

Furnishing clients with fine wines and outstanding French cuisine, the enterprising temptress could command up to $1,000 a night for her company.

Not afraid to flaunt her wealth, Julia traveled around town in a lacquered carriage sporting a crest with four aces, and she had her own box at the theatre. But she was also known to contribute food and clothing to poor families and widows of miners killed in accidents, and when an epidemic swept through Virginia City, she nursed ill men in her parlor house.

In recognition of her civic-mindedness, Julia was made an honorary member of the Virginia City Fire Company, which transported her through the streets on a fire wagon during a Fourth of July parade.

But on Sunday morning, January 29, 1867, Julia was found murdered in her bed, bludgeoned and strangled to death, apparently for her jewelry. Virginia City shut down for her funeral, and the procession was the largest in community history.

Several weeks later, a man by the name of John Millain was caught with several of the stolen items, and on February 27, Virginia City was closed down again—this time to witness his execution.

Top left: "The Castle" was built on B Street in 1868 by mine superintendent Robert N. Graves. **Above:** The three-story Mackey Mansion faced D Street, which was level with the second floor. John Mackey's mine offices were on the lower level.

Tourists take a ride on the vintage equipment of the Virginia & Truckee Railroad, which was completed in 1869 and over the next 70 years hauled millions of dollars worth of silver and gold from the Comstock Lode. A century ago, as many as 45 trains per day arrived and departed Virginia City.

DELTA SALOON'S SUICIDE TABLE

The Delta Saloon, today one of Virginia City's most popular tourist attractions, exhibits a faro table that proved so deadly to its owners that it became known as the "Suicide Table."

Although it has now disappeared, faro was the most popular game in Western saloons and casinos because of its low house percentage (the reason it is no longer dealt).

The infamous table was brought to Virginia City in the early 1860s, but the first owner, one "Black Jake," lost $70,000 in one evening and shot himself. The second owner ran the table for only one disastrous night. Unable to cover his losses, he either committed suicide or was shot by an unhappy winner.

No dealer would play this unlucky table, and it was stored for several decades. During the late 1890s, however, it was put back into play as a blackjack table. One stormy night, a miner who had been cleaned out in another gambling house came in and tried his luck. The miner won—and continued to win. By the end of the night, the dealer had lost $86,000, a team of horses, and an interest in a gold mine. Having lost everything, the dealer committed suicide.

Spread photo: Looking north on C Street today. At right is the Bucket of Blood Saloon, and across the street is the Delta Saloon. The open space on the left side of the street behind the telephone pole at center was the site of the six-story International Hotel.

TONOPAH
NEVADA

At the base of Sawtooth Peak in the harsh desert of western Nevada was an old Indian campground called Tonopah (from the Shoshone word for "water brush," a small desert shrub). On May 18, 1900, a 45-year-old prospector known as "Lazy Jim" Butler camped at the site.

Three days earlier he had left his wife, Belle, at their ranch north of Belmont, heading south for Southern Klondike, a mining camp 15 miles below Tonopah. The next morning Butler had to chase a burro that had strayed during the night, and when he spotted the missing animal, he angrily picked up a rock. Instead of flinging the rock, however, he examined the mineral flecks in it with a practiced eye.

Butler chiseled out more samples, and back at the Southern Klondike he offered assayer Fred Hicks a quarter-interest for an $8 assay of his find. When Hicks declined the offer, Butler returned to

The elevator hoistworks of one of the old mines overlooking Tonopah. The district tallied $9.6 million worth of gold in 1913, the peak production year.

A more recent hoistworks on the southwest edge of Tonopah. The five-story Mizpah Hotel is visible at the far left, with Mt. Oddie rising up behind it.

"Lazy Jim" Butler and his burro, "Me." The 45-year-old prospector discovered gold while camping at Tonopah in 1900; he staked out a number of claims that would become rich mines.

Tonopah, then journeyed back to Belmont with his 75 pounds of ore. Eventually, Tasker Oddie, a young lawyer in Belmont who had succeeded Butler as district attorney, agreed to assay his friend's ore. But Oddie, like Butler, was cash-strapped and promised another friend, Walter Gayhart, half of his quarter-interest for an assay. Gayhart, the high school principal at Austin, assayed as a sideline and took his time about testing the Butler samples.

As fate would have it, the assay promised rich amounts of both silver and gold, and Gayhart, Oddie, and the Butlers headed for Tonopah to make their fortunes. Gayhart laid out the townsite and became wealthy in real estate. Oddie prospered, saw Sawtooth Peak renamed Mount Oddie in his honor, and went on to serve Nevada as governor and U.S. senator.

The camp was christened Butler City, although Tonopah soon became the official label. Lazy Jim staked out several claims that became rich mines, including the Mizpah, destined to become the most productive in the Tonopah District.

Tonopah was isolated and waterless, and the only way Butler could develop his promising claims was to lease them. In return for 25 percent of their proceeds, Butler gave miners until the last day of 1901 to produce as much ore as possible.

Most of the leasers realized large profits, several earned fortunes, and there was a riotous celebration when the lease agreements expired on December 31. The Butlers became wealthy early in 1902, when the Tonopah Mining Company of Eastern investors bought the Mizpah and other rich claims.

As the town began to grow, frame structures were dragged in from other towns and aligned along the wide north-south Main Street that recently had been Sawtooth Pass. The *Tonopah Bonanza* began publication in June of 1901, and soon there were two more newspapers. Before long, the town had three banks, as well as a stock exchange. The Butler Theater headlined vaudeville shows, the Opera House featured a roller skating rink, and the so-called Big Casino offered all kinds of adult entertainment.

A dance hall that was the center of Tonopah's tenderloin district, the Big Casino was also a plush betting parlor with a wire service that provided bookmaking on races and other sporting events nationwide.

By the end of 1902 there were 32 saloons, the most popular of which became the Tonopah Club.

There was a three-day celebration when a railroad connection reached Tonopah in July of 1904, and the next year a courthouse erected as the seat of Nye County was moved in from the town of Belmont. Millions of dollars worth of ore was being removed annually from the mines, driving the population of Tonopah past 20,000.

The Tonopah boom initiated a series of bonanzas across western Nevada, most notably in Goldfield in 1902 and in Rhyolite two years later. These strikes of the early 20th century reversed a serious decline in Nevada's economy and population.

Nevada was granted statehood in 1864 on the heels of the discovery of the Comstock Lode around Virginia City. The Comstock's peak of production was achieved in the 1870s, and Nevada's population climbed to 62,226, according to the census of 1880. But mining activities fell off badly during the next two decades, causing a substantial population dropoff, to 42,355, by 1900. Amid growing talk of depriving Nevada of statehood, mineral discoveries were made at Tonopah and succeeding sites, rejuvenating the state as a new century began.

The Montana-Tonopah Mine in 1903. Tonopah founder Jim Butler and his wife Belle Butler are standing in the center. Butler leased many of his valuable claims, closing each deal with a handshake rather than a written contract.

Unfortunately, Tonopah, along with Goldfield, became plagued with labor difficulties, as strikes were organized by the I.W.W. (Industrial Workers of the World, or "Wobblies"). Production peaked in 1913 at $9.6 million, then began a decline that took a heavy toll on Tonopah. The mines continued producing, however, sometimes yielding more than $1 million in a good year.

At least 2,000 people continued to inhabit Tonopah, and the population tripled during World War II when an air base was established east of town. But the population nosedived at war's end, especially after the railroad was closed in 1947.

During the late 1960s, billionaire Howard Hughes, convinced that ample bullion still existed beneath Tonopah, bought dozens of gold and silver mines at bargain rates. There was little development, however, and the Hughes properties went on sale during the 1970s.

Today, Tonopah survives as a tourist town—and as a mecca for history buffs interested in Western Americana.

The Big Casino Dance Hall in 1909, with conductor Jules Goldschmidt posing in front of dancers and his house band.

Tonopah in March of 1907. The five-story Mizpah Hotel dominated the upper part of town, while the Big Casino anchored the tenderloin district on lower Main Street. When the Big Casino opened each afternoon, trumpeters walked outside to play what locals termed "the call of the wild."

Top Photo: Ore ready for shipment from the Tonopah freight yard. (Note silhouette of photographer in foreground.) **Bottom photo:** Nevada Governor Tasker Oddie (right) and his niece at the christening of the Battleship Nevada. As a young lawyer, Oddie helped found Tonopah, and he lent his name to the mountain beside the new town.

Old granary afflicted with a precipitous lean. Farmers and ranchers who resisted the lure of gold and silver could capitalize on the voracious demand for agricultural products.

THE MARVELOUS
MIZPAH

In 1907, booming Tonopah boasted three banks, three newspapers, several theatres, and a number of lodging houses, but not one first-class hotel. To remedy the situation, the Mizpah Saloon & Grill, a single-story frame building, was moved to another site to make room for "the finest hotel in the district."

The new, five-story Mizpah Hotel rapidly rose above Tonopah, but in December of 1907, the effects of a nationwide financial panic caused construction money to disappear. The Mizpah was boarded up until the following summer, when building crews were put back on the job.

At the Mizpah's grand opening in November of 1908, some 5,000 people came to admire the suites, meeting rooms, steam heat, and other modern amenities of the new hotel.

Opened in 1908 at a cost of $200,000, the five-story Mizpah Hotel is still the most impressive building in Tonopah.

"Nor does the weary one have to climb stairs," gushed one reporter, "for an electric elevator runs from basement or garret, and should the guest desire, he can stroll into the office, state that he wants to be fed, bathed, and put into bed, and all these things will be attended to for him."

The Mizpah offered its "high standard of excellence" for only a few years before Tonopah went into decline. Like the town itself, the hotel underwent a slow but inevitable deterioration as the decades passed.

In 1976, Las Vegas millionaire Frank Scott, who had fallen in love with the Mizpah in the 1930s, bought the old hotel and funded a three-year restoration at a cost of $4 million. The "Marvelous Mizpah" reopened in glory in 1979, just in time for a new mining boom in the 1980s.

Today, the hotel is a popular stop for history buffs and vacationers alike.

A busy gathering at the Mizpah Hotel during the 1920s. Considered the finest hotel in the district when it opened in 1908, the hotel became known as the "Marvelous Mizpah."

The setting sun casts an unusual glow upon the desert landscape surrounding Tonopah.

Wild horses at Alkali Spring, 11 miles south of Tonopah. Herds of mustangs, descended from horses of early Spanish explorers, still roam the enormous Nevada ranges.

GOLDFIELD
NEVADA

In 1902, prospectors Billy Marsh and Harry Stimler staked out several claims in the barren, volcanic desert of western Nevada, establishing a mining camp that came to be called Grandpa. When it was eventually learned that, except for Colorado's Cripple Creek, the area's best ore had the highest concentration of gold in the entire United States, the town was rechristened Goldfield, a fitting name for one of the West's last gold-mining towns.

Goldfield exploded with growth as prospectors, promoters, miners, merchants, gamblers, prostitutes, and other Western adventurers of the early 20th century came to a site they hoped would offer one more great bonanza like those of the 19th century. By 1906, business lots sold for $45,000, and civic leaders attempted to promote population growth—and the sale of mine shares on Goldfield's

Just beyond the old Ford building is the four-story Goldfield Hotel, which opened in 1910.

A dilapidated stone house (foreground) provides a sharp contrast to Goldfield's handsome school (background).

The discovery of gold in 1902 turned Goldfield into one of the last Western boomtowns. This early photo shows a lively commercial district that includes a jewelry store, bank, theater, hotel, restaurant, and horse market.

own stock exchange—by any means necessary, including such outlandish proposals as digging a pool on Main Street and keeping it filled with beer.

The most ingenious boost to Goldfield came from the fertile imagination of George Lewis "Tex" Rickard, majority owner of the Northern Saloon, which boasted of being "the biggest sporting house in America." A lifelong gambler and adventurer who had cowboyed in Texas, worn a marshal's badge, and sought gold in the Klondike, Rickard put Goldfield on the map with a spectacular boxing promotion.

Utilizing his own assets and raising money from members of the Goldfield Club (an athletic organization) and other wealthy sportsmen, Rickard offered a $30,000 purse for a championship boxing match between Oscar Matthew "Battling" Nelson and Joe Gans. Rickard ostentatiously displayed the purse—the largest ever for a prizefight—in stacks of $20 gold pieces in the window of a Goldfield bank. The fight was advertised by flooding the sporting public with nearly 70,000 promotional letters and postcards and by releasing dispatches to the nation's newspapers describing the "daily quarrel" between the pugilists.

This energetic publicity campaign focused the nation's attention on Goldfield. Scheduled for Labor Day of 1906, the fight pitted Nelson, a 24-year-old native of Denmark who specialized in low blows, butting ("I was only rubbin' my hair in his eyes") and other dirty tactics, against Joe Gans, a black boxer from Baltimore who was nearly 30 and who had thrown several fights.

There was heavy betting on both men. Even at ringside, miners wagered sacks of nuggets and mining claims. Gans outboxed Nelson for 10 rounds, whereupon Nelson began to butt, gouge, and trip his more skillful opponent. In the 32nd round, Gans broke a bone in his left hand, but he fought on gamely until the 42nd round, when Nelson floored him with one of his patented blows to the groin. The referee disqualified Nelson, and even though Rickard had bet on the loser, he earned more than $13,000 on a $60,000 gate. Within a few years, he would become the nation's most famous fight promoter.

Rickard's publicity stunt helped the population of Goldfield soar past 20,000. The four-story Goldfield Hotel, completed at a cost of $500,000 in 1910, opened with a three-day party. The most prominent saloon, one of the largest anywhere in the West, was the Northern, boasting a massive bar that required dozens of bartenders.

In a raw incident reminiscent of the 19th-century frontier, a brawl broke out over a faro game in the Northern on the night of May 25, 1905. The four gamblers battled their way outside, whereupon John Redmond opened fire with a revolver, shattering the knee of an innocent bystander.

Goldfield did not soon settle down. At five o'clock on the morning of February 1, 1909, for example, three masked men boldly walked into the crowded Mohawk Saloon and at gunpoint looted the cash register and safe of $3,417.

Violent measures were used to curtail theft, such as the repeated robbery in 1907 of amalgam, a valuable mercury alloy used in reducing ore. A trap was set at the Nevada-Goldfield Re-

This monument commemorates the widely ballyhooed Gans-Nelson prizefight, staged in 1906 by Tex Rickard, who became the nation's foremost fight promoter. The $30,000 purse was displayed in stacks of $20 gold pieces in the window of a Goldfield bank.

duction Works, and when a thief appeared and began to collect amalgam he was shot four times in the head. The dying robber was identified as V. L. Kline, the "highly esteemed" proprietor of one of the largest jewelry stores in Goldfield.

Mine superintendents who hired gunmen to counter amalgam theft were not inclined to tolerate strikes. When miners went on strike in December of 1907, influential mine owners brought federal troops to Goldfield, imported strikebreakers from out of state, and quickly saw mine operations return to normal.

An estimated $150 million in gold came out of the Goldfield District. Production peaked in 1910,

when the take was $11 million, but two years later the annual output dropped to $5 million. In 1918 it plummeted to $1.5 million, then to just $750,000 the next year.

The population dropped almost as rapidly as it had grown, and when fire raged through Goldfield on July 7, 1923, most of the buildings it destroyed had already been abandoned. Many of the masonry structures survived, however, most notably the Goldfield Hotel. In recent years there have been unsuccessful attempts to reopen the historic property, and perhaps one day tourists and ghost town buffs will again be able to enjoy its antique hospitality.

By 1906, commercial lots in Goldfield were priced at $45,000, and the population soon soared past 20,000.

The sign on this Goldfield building—"There is gold in them thar hills"—was abundantly true. Mines of the district produced an estimated $150 million worth of gold.

THE ART OF
HIGH-GRADING

Hard-rock miners considered "high-grading" a fringe benefit. With wages of no more than $4 a day for dangerous, backbreaking work, miners often supplemented their incomes by bringing home a few pounds of high-grade ore.

Ore was highly concentrated in Goldfield mines. In the Mohawk Mine, for example, an 8-inch-thick seam was valued at $250,000 a ton, making a single pound of ore worth $125, more than a miner earned in a month. Goldfield miners developed high-grading into an art, through the years making off with an estimated $30 million in ore.

At the end of a workday, a miner could carry out three or four pounds of ore in his lunch pail. When the shift foreman or superintendent began to check

A prospector displays the tools of his trade, which in this case included two cap-and-ball revolvers. Thieves, claim jumpers, and hostile Indians were a real threat to miners everywhere.

lunch pails, miners began to carry out their booty in false-crowned hats or vest-like, multipocketed garments worn beneath their shirts. Miners' wives often sewed long canvas pockets inside the legs of pants. Management countered by building "change-houses"

and requiring miners to exchange their muddy work clothes for clean clothing.

Miners who were caught were rarely convicted by juries comprised of fellow miners and local merchants dependent upon their trade. Likewise, mine superintendents striving for rapid production faced the possibility of work slowdowns if they tried to curtail the practice.

Mine owners attempted to reduce high-grading by persuading a local preacher to emphasize the commandment against theft. Still, the practice continued. It was common knowledge that many Goldfield miners worked not so much for their daily wages but for what they might bring out concealed.

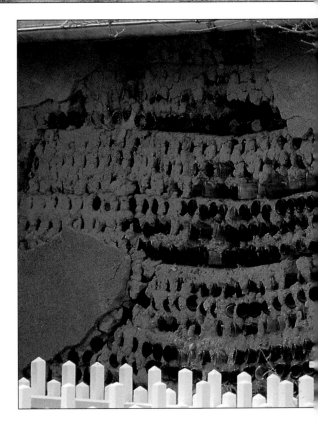

Far left: Old elevator hoist at one of the mines in the Goldfield District. **Left:** Mining towns were filled with narrow "shotgun" houses—so named because a gun could be fired through the front door and out the back without hitting anything. **Below:** More unique housing was this residence built with beer bottles.

TRAPPED IN A
CAVE-IN!

Thousands of miners ended up being buried alive in underground shafts and tunnels across the West, and heroic efforts were expended to rescue them.

Early in their shift in a Goldfield mine, 20 men were entombed by the sudden collapse of 400 feet of their tunnel. One of the miners, Frank Crampton, later testified that there wasn't a man among them who wasn't "scared stiff."

Although water constantly dripped from the rock walls, the tunnel sloped and allowed the water to drain. Clothing would stay wet, but there would be little water to drink. The cave-in had occurred before mealtime, so there were 20 lunch pails to be rationed.

The trapped men soon heard the blasting of a rescue party, but on the third day a concussion knocked out their candles and carbide lamps. All matches were water-soaked, and the remaining 11 days would be spent in total darkness. "But with darkness," related Crampton, "sounds from our watches were as loud as a boiler factory in which a drum corps was practicing." Crampton collected the watches and dropped them into a hole.

Hunger and bone-chilling dampness tormented the miners. One of the men went berserk and ran screaming into the darkness to his death. Although the 19 survivors lost all track of time, on the fourteenth day they heard a noise nearby and then the welcome voice of a rescuer: "Cover up your eyes, here we come with lights!"

AURORA
NEVADA

On August 21, 1860, a trio of prospectors found promising ore samples several miles east of the California mining town of Bodie. James Braley and E. R. Hicks deferred to their well-read partner, J. M. Corey, in naming the campsite "Aurora, Goddess of the Dawn" and the 100-square-mile mining district surrounding it "Esmerelda" (a word he came to admire while reading French novelist Victor Hugo).

Within two months Aurora was a booming tent city, and the founders quickly sold their claims: Corey and Braley settled in Santa Clara, California, with $30,000 apiece, while Hicks headed for his native Arkansas with an estimated $10,000 in his pocket.

Aurora was located at an altitude exceeding 7,700 feet just inside, it was thought, the eastern border of California. Anticipating large tax revenues from the new

Foundation of a stamp mill located 2 miles northeast of Aurora.

In 1912, a new mining area was opened just over the hill from Aurora, and a small company town, Mangum, sprang up for a few years.

Undated photo shows Aurora's main street after years of abandonment. Eventually, the town's brick structures were demolished for their building materials.

mining district, the California legislature hastily organized Mono County in March of 1861, naming Aurora the county seat. But when the Nevada Territory was created the next year, the new territorial assembly made Aurora the seat of Esmerelda County.

This meant that litigation could be taken either to Esmerelda County's Judge Turner or to Mono County's Judge Baldwin. For voting purposes, Aurora residents could register in Nevada or California or both, and they could vote Democratic at Armory Hall on the Nevada edge of town, or Republican on the California side of Aurora. This unique voting situation lasted only until September of 1863, when an official survey placed Aurora three miles inside the Nevada line. By that time, the town had 3,000 residents.

Business lots sold from $2,500 to $5,000, and there were 22 saloons and more than 20 stores, as well as lodging houses, newspapers, two churches, numerous brothels, and various other enterprises. By the spring of 1864, 17 stamp mills had been erected.

During the Civil War, Aurora became a center for Confederate sympathizers, although most citizens supported the Union. Pro-Confederate displays were countered by two Union companies that drilled at Armory Hall: the Esmerelda Rangers, a cavalry troop; and the Hooker Rifles, an infantry unit.

Mines in the Esmerelda District were less than 100 feet deep, but by 1865, $24 million in gold and silver had been extracted. Aurora's population had vaulted to 6,000, and some estimates went as high as 10,000. But the shallow bonanzas rapidly played out, and just as rapidly the miners scattered to new strike areas. In 1883, the county seat was moved to Hawthorne, and Aurora's post office closed in 1897.

Several years later, however, the development of cyanide processing resulted in the reopening of Esmerelda's best mines. In 1912, a cyanide plant and a 40-stamp mill were built, and a small company town named Mangum was established just over the hill from Aurora.

The company prohibited liquor, so several saloons—the Aurora Club, the First and Last Chance Saloon, the Tunnel Saloon, the Elite Bar, and the Northern—were opened in Aurora. This revival ended in 1917, when the plant, mill, and other buildings were closed and dismantled.

During the 1920s, many of the abandoned structures of Aurora were sold and moved. Eventually, even Aurora's big masonry structures were broken up for their bricks, and today only their foundations—and the town cemetery—remain at the remote town site.

Left: Mark Twain. At the age of 25, Samuel Clemens traveled west with his brother Orion, who had been appointed secretary to the territorial governor of Nevada. Clemens adventurously tried to develop mining properties in Aurora, but lack of success as a prospector turned him to journalism under the pen name Mark Twain. **Below:** A buggy ride for children of Aurora.

All that remains of Aurora today are its building foundations and the old cemetery. **Opposite page:** California's Risdon Iron Works provided machinery during the revival of mining activity around Aurora.

SWIFT JUSTICE IN
AURORA

"All quiet and orderly. Four men will be hanged in half an hour."

The above message was telegraphed to an anxious Governor James W. Nye on February 9, 1864, on behalf of 600 Aurora men who comprised the recently organized Citizens' Protective Committee.

The group was formed to take back the town from increasingly bold lawless elements that were terrorizing the citizenry. At least 27 men had been slain in Aurora in recent months.

The latest victim was W. R. Rogers, brutally murdered because he had participated in the shooting death of horse thief James Sears. Rogers was shot by James Daley, the 25-year-old leader of Aurora's underworld, then his throat was cut by William Buckley. Accomplices "Three-Fingered Jack" McDowell and James Masterson rifled his pockets and set his clothes on fire.

It was one outrage too many. Within hours after Rogers' murder, hundreds of men formed a vigilante committee. Attendance at Rogers' funeral was enormous, and during the next few days his four killers and several other known outlaws were arrested. A gallows was built beside Armory Hall.

Daley's last request was for all the brandy he could drink, and when he mounted the scaffold he drunkenly cursed the crowd. Of the four condemned men, Buckley was the most courageous. He paid for his own coffin, refused liquor, dictated a letter to his brother, and admitted his guilt. "All you boys must come to my wake tonight in John Daley's cabin," he urged. "Goodbye, and God bless you all."

GRAFTON
UTAH

Grafton is the most picturesque ghost town in Utah and one of the most photographed towns in the West. A Mormon colony settled before the Civil War, it suffered Indian attacks and destructive floods, finally being abandoned early in the 20th century.

The rustic old town set against a spectacular mountain was eventually discovered by Hollywood. Beginning in 1950, several Western movies were filmed in Grafton, including the 1969 blockbuster, *Butch Cassidy and the Sundance Kid.*

Named after a pioneer settler, Grafton was built on the south bank of the Virgin River. Late in 1861, torrential rains besieged the area, and in January of 1862, following 40 days without letup, a powerful flood swept Grafton downriver. A few miles away, the citizens of a town called Virgin stood on high ground and watched portions of the town float by on the swollen river.

Built in 1886 with donated labor, Grafton's adobe school doubled as a Mormon meeting house.

After Hollywood began filming Westerns in Grafton during the 1950s, the ghost town's five surviving buildings were shored up and sometimes supplemented with movie-set fronts.

Grafton was rebuilt nearly two miles upstream, and soon large numbers of new settlers arrived in the area. Meanwhile, in Salt Lake City, Brigham Young directed more than 300 Mormon "units" to colonize Dixie, the name given to an area of southern Utah because it was suitable for growing cotton.

The Mormons established a cluster of Dixie communities that included Grafton. By 1864, nearly 30 families (168 people) in Grafton cultivated cotton and planted orchards, producing apples, peaches, cherries, pears, berries, grapes, and currants. These industrious colonists dug more than 7 miles of canals and ditches to work 200 productive acres.

Because of the constant danger of Indian attack, the men worked the fields with loaded guns nearby. The Grafton cemetery became the final resting place for many who died from arrow wounds.

When Indian raids abated in the 1870s, Grafton and nearby communities imported silkworm eggs and began producing silk. Grafton women were able to replace uncomfortable homespun with luxurious silk dresses. By this time, settlers were also raising sheep and cattle.

Grafton boasted a church, a school, a post office, and a variety of log, frame, and adobe residences. But flooding problems persisted, and after the turn of the century the population declined rapidly. In 1921, with only three families in residence, Grafton ceased to be part of the Mormon Church and was soon deserted.

But three decades later, film crews began to arrive, stabilizing the most substantial of the surviving structures and sometimes putting up temporary saloon and storefronts. In 1969, millions of movie fans saw Butch Cassidy and the Sundance Kid (Paul Newman and Robert Redford) visit schoolmarm Etta Place (Katherine Ross) at old Grafton.

Nestled in the shadow of Zion National Park, Grafton is hard to reach, but well worth the effort. It remains one of the West's most fascinating ghost towns.

After the farmers of Grafton began producing silk with imported silkworm eggs, women of the community replaced homespun garments with silk dresses.

Looking down Grafton's deserted main street toward the adobe school. Overhanging branches are from mulberry trees, planted because the leaves are a natural food of silkworms.

John Wood's brick house was built just down the street from Grafton's school. In the background are Mount Kinesava and Zion National Park.

MARVELOUS FLOOD
TENNEY

Looking south at Grafton across the Virgin River. The town was plagued by flooding problems.

In January of 1862, after 40 miserable days of almost constant rain, Utah's Virgin River went on an awesome rampage.

While poorly situated Grafton was being engulfed in flood waters, the young wife of Nathan Tenney went into labor with the couple's first child. The rushing torrents would not wait for the birth to be completed, and water began to swirl into the Tenney cabin.

Several men courageously waded through knee-deep water to help Nathan place the expectant mother into a wagon bed. Then they shoved, floated, and lifted the makeshift maternity ward to higher ground, where without further complications a son was born. It wasn't long before the cabin was swept away, but everyone involved in the birth and rescue got out of harm's way in time.

In honor of his memorable debut, the baby was named Marvelous Flood Tenney.

BODIE
CALIFORNIA

Bodie was one of the most lawless mining camps on the frontier, for a time averaging six murders a week; today, it survives as what many consider California's finest ghost town.

Despite destructive blazes in 1892 and 1932, more than 150 weathered structures await the adventurer willing to journey 13 miles along a gravel road to a remote valley on the eastern slope of the Sierra Nevada. The only residents today are state park employees, but the deserted old town once rocked with raucous music, bawdy laughter—and gunfire.

California's original gold strike was on the western slope of the Sierra Nevada mountain range, but in the fall of 1859, prospector Bill Bodey and three partners found paydirt at the site that would eventually bear an altered spelling of his name.

The four men agreed to come back the following spring, but

Overview of Bodie. Miners' hall is at left. Structure just above center of photo, at the end of the street, was the town's Methodist Church.

The two-story building with the false front was the Odd Fellows Lodge, built in 1878. The Bodie Athletic Club also met there.

View of Bodie from the Standard Mine. Despite fires in 1892 and 1932—and more than a century of severe winter weather—at least 150 structures still survive.

Bodey returned within weeks with a miner named Taylor. They built a log cabin and began to work the diggings, until Bodey was caught in a blizzard and froze to death. During the spring thaw, Taylor buried Bodey where he found the body, although the remains were reinterred in the Bodie cemetery two decades later. A year after Bodey's death, Taylor was killed and scalped by a Paiute war party.

For a decade and a half, Bodie was a small mining camp with only a couple of dozen cabins.

All of that changed in 1876, when a cave-in at the Bunker Hill Mine revealed a rich gold vein. By the next year, 2,000 people had rushed to Bodie.

Another discovery in 1878 produced ore that assayed at $1,000 per ton, boosting the population past 10,000. Soon, Bodie's main street was a mile long, with three newspapers—the *Daily Free Press,* the *Free Union,* and the *Weekly Standard*—recording the boomtown's activities.

The residents of Bodie led a hard existence, especially during the bitter winters. (Mark Twain

A three-legged race on Bodie's main street during a Fourth of July celebration. Races between volunteer fire companies also were favorite holiday events.

described Bodie's weather cycle as "the breakup of one winter and the beginning of the next.") The large population, as well as more than two dozen mines and numerous other businesses, went through 45,000 cords of wood a year, which provided employment to 2,000 woodcutters and teamsters.

Freight wagons and burro trains hauled the wood along rugged mountain trails until 1881, when the Bodie Railway and Lumber Company spent $600,000 to build 32 miles of track to a 12,000-acre timber supply near Mono Lake. The narrow gauge railroad carried only firewood and lumber.

The railway was built by Chinese laborers, and Bodie had a larger Chinese population than any other American city except San Francisco. The Chinese operated a variety of enterprises, including restaurants, laundries, and opium dens. The latter complemented Bodie's 65 saloons, which included Pat Fahey's, the Maison Dore, and the Philadelphia Beer Depot. Additional entertainment was available along intentionally misnamed Virgin Alley and Maiden Lane, where Bodie's red-light district was centered.

The vault of what used to be Bodie Bank continues to defy time and the forces of nature. Most of the structure was destroyed by fire in 1932.

Frequent gunfights and robberies accounted for a large number of shooting deaths. For years, the *Sacramento Union* stationed a reporter in Bodie to keep its readers entertained with the most recent crimes. Young Mark Twain, covering one particularly bloody incident for Virginia City's *Territorial Enterprise*, was duly impressed by the carnage: "The smoke of battle almost never clears away completely in Bodie."

Of course, criminal activity wasn't the only cause of unnatural death in Bodie. Following is an excerpt from a letter received by one of the town's early newspapers:

"I see in the paper that a man named John Sipes was attacted and et up by a bare whose kubs he was trying to get to when the she bare came up and stopt him by eating him in the mountains near your town. What I want to know is, did it kill him ded or was he only partly et up, and is he from this plaice and all about the bare. I don't know but he is a distant husband of mine. My first husband was of that name and I supposed he was killed in the war, but the name of

Top photo: Gasoline pumps and abandoned trucks are reminders that some mining activity continued during the early decades of the 20th century. **Bottom photo:** A California state park since 1964, Bodie remains in essentially the same condition as when the last occupants departed.

the man the bare et being the same I thought it might be him after all . . . If it is him you will know it by his having six toes on his left foot . . . Find out all you kin about him without him knowing what it is for, that is if the bare did not eat him all up. If it did I don't see as you kin do anything and you needn't to trouble . . ."

The situation in Bodie began to change after 1881, when mining production dropped rapidly and people began leaving town. Water in the shafts became a serious problem, and soon only six mines were in operation.

Bodie experienced a partial revival in the 1890s with the advent of a cyanide process of extracting gold from mine tailings, but it only forestalled the inevitable. Mining came to a complete halt before World War II. By that time, Bodie was abandoned, but the isolation helped protect the buildings of what is today considered a truly superb ghost town.

The sun hitting the rooftops of Bodie's historic buildings creates a beautiful array of textures. Maintained in a state of arrested decay, the old mining town became a California state park in 1964.

Top photo: Time seems to have stopped in this Bodie kitchen. **Bottom photo:** Lobby of one of the many hotels that housed visitors when Bodie was in its prime.

Interior of the Boone store. Opium was sold across the counter in many of Bodie's stores. The enterprising Boone also operated a livery stable.

Interior of Sam Leone's Bar and Casino, one of 65 such establishments in rowdy Bodie.

GOODBYE, GOD...
HELLO, BODIE!

"Goodbye, God, we're moving to Bodie," prayed a frightened little girl after learning that her family was relocating there.

The unintentionally humorous quote appeared in a Sacramento newspaper story about the lawlessness that plagued the California mining town. Bodie's own *Free Union* countered with an editorial insisting that what the girl actually said was, "Good! By God, we're moving to Bodie!" However, even a brief study of the newspaper's back issues suggests that God may have indeed forsaken the remote frontier community.

During a typical three-day period, for example, there were three murders. One week there were four stagecoach robberies, but a fifth holdup was foiled by Wells Fargo guards who killed three highwaymen. One pair of industrious robbers held up two stagecoaches outside Bodie during a single day.

In 1880, two Mexicans intercepted a coach outside Bodie and stole $30,000 in gold bullion. Chased down by a posse, one bandit was killed by the pursuers, while the other died that night in the Bodie jail—without ever revealing the location of the money.

At a dance on January 14, 1881, Joseph DeRoche quarreled with a man named Treloar over the latter's wife. When DeRoche shot Treloar in the back after the dance, he was taken to jail, but a 200-man mob seized DeRoche and hanged him.

There were enough troublemakers in Bodie to keep its jail occupied, but prisoners were not always secure from lynch mobs.

During one particularly violent fortnight, one man was shot to death, one woman's skull was crushed with a club, a man and a woman were stabbed, and two men were severely pistol-whipped. Shooting victim John Rann met his maker at the bar of Wagner's Beer Parlor, but another saloon shootout between a bartender, an angry patron, and a gambler whose cigar was shot from his mouth produced nothing more than a grazed scalp.

More typical of Bodie, however, was the brawl between Dave Bannon and Ed Ryan. Unable to resolve their differences, they grabbed each other by the neck and fatally shot each other through the torso. All things considered, Bodie was not a good place to get into an argument.

HORNITOS
CALIFORNIA

Named for the unusual "tombs" of its earliest residents, the sleepy California town of Hornitos became a lively—sometimes dangerous—place after the forty-niners arrived.

The Mexican people who first settled here found the ground too hard to dig standard graves, so they developed the practice of placing coffins in shallow depressions scraped into the earth. Stones were then stacked tightly around the containers, which were topped with slab roofs. These grave coverings resembled small versions of outdoor baking ovens—*hornos* in Spanish—and so they came to be called "little ovens," or *hornitos.*

The town grew quickly as mining activity increased. The nearby Jenny Lind Mine built the district's first stamp mill in 1851. Other big mines near Hornitos were the Mount Gaines and the Ruth Pierce, and a few miles away was the wild mining camp of Quartzburg.

Every type of wagon was pressed into service to transport ore from California during the Gold Rush.

Built in 1862, St. Catherine's Catholic Church still serves Hornitos and is one of the town's best-preserved historic buildings.

Hornitos in 1917, looking south toward the plaza. During its wildest era, Hornitos supported 34 saloons, plus numerous opium dens in the Chinese section just beyond the plaza.

Mrs. Merck, a saloon operator, had a reputation for maintaining at least a semblance of order in her bar. Born in France, she became known as "the grand dame of Hornitos."

When vigilantes in Quartzburg angrily chased the prostitutes, pickpockets, card-sharks, and other undesireables out of town, most of these exiles moved to Hornitos, adding to the rough elements already present.

Soon there were 34 saloons in Hornitos, and numerous opium dens in the Chinese section just north of the old plaza. Legendary outlaw Joaquin Murieta frequented the dives of Hornitos, once escaping arrest by scurrying through a tunnel used to move beer barrels from a storeroom to a dance hall.

Writer Bret Harte described Hornitos as a town "where everything that loathes the law found congenial soil and flourished." Neverthe-less, solid citizens battled for control of their community, some forming vigilante groups to fight against outlawry.

After a meeting of a miners' court in May 1851 at Rattlesnake Ike's Saloon, for example, the *Hornitos Times* was authorized to run the following public notice: "All citizens of Hornitos are respectfully invited to attend the hanging of Cherokee Bill, horse thief."

That same year, a small but sturdy stone jail was built in the center of town. After a Chinese man was jailed there for shooting an Anglo, he was lured to a window near the ceiling with an offer of food. Suddenly the prisoner was seized, then promptly strangled to death by a rope lowered through the bars.

Citizens of Hornitos pose in front of Reeb's Butcher Shop on the plaza around 1880. **Below:** Aboveground burial was practiced by early Mexican residents. Their little rock mounds resembled ovens (*hornos* in Spanish), so when the town was formed it was named Hornitos ("little ovens") after these structures.

A Masonic lodge was organized by solid citizens of the town, and a new Catholic church was built in 1862. The two-story Hornitos Hotel entertained a respectable clientele, and D. Ghirardelli opened a mercantile store that would eventually establish him as San Francisco's "chocolate king."

By the time the mines closed, Hornitos was an orderly community by most measures, and the cemetery surrounding the Catholic church had far outgrown Dead Man's Gulch, Hornitos' version of Boot Hill. Today the church still stands, and so do the Masonic Hall, the ruins of Ghirardelli's store, the jail, the hotel, the Wells Fargo office, and many other structures of the Mother Lode's best ghost town.

Above: The stone walls of the Hornitos jail were two feet thick, and iron rings were imbedded in the floor for securing leg irons. **Right:** The remains of the D. Ghirardelli store remind visitors that the celebrated San Francisco chocolate magnate got his start in Hornitos.

BANDIT AND HERO
JOAQUIN MURIETA

During California's gold rush era, there were at least five Mexican outlaws who were known by the name Joaquin, including Joaquin Murieta, who received much of the blame for crimes of the other Joaquins and who eventually became an infamous composite of all of them.

Born in Sonora, Mexico, in 1830, Murieta was attracted to California by the gold rush, but after being subjected to racial discrimination and arrest, he began to commit acts of retaliation. Murieta was a highwayman, but he was also a hero to the Mexican people, and Hornitos was a favorite hangout. His gang made raids throughout the San Joaquin Valley, hiding on the ranches of old *Californios* who had been unfairly displaced by white settlers.

Large rewards were offered for his capture, and on July 25, 1853, Captain Harry Love and 20 California Rangers ambushed the outlaw's camp, killing Joaquin and seven other men who were part of his gang. Murieta's head was severed and placed in a glass jar filled with whiskey, then taken to Hornitos for identification by Joaquin's cronies.

Although there were persistent claims that the so-called "Ghost of Sonora" actually escaped the gun battle and lived until at least 1878, the preserved head was displayed in a San Francisco museum until it was destroyed by the great earthquake and fire of 1906.

THE NORTHWEST

SILVER CITY
IDAHO

The "Queen of the Owyhee," Silver City produced enormous amounts of silver and gold ore, then drifted into obscurity and became the queen of Idaho ghost towns.

Getting to Silver City requires negotiating a 23-mile gravel road with countless switchbacks, but the adventurous traveler is rewarded with one of the most picturesque and atmospheric ghost towns in the West.

In May of 1863, Michael Jordan led 28 fellow prospectors out of Placerville, Idaho, in search of the Blue Bucket Diggings, a legendary gold field rumored to exist in the Owyhee Mountains of southwestern Idaho. Struggling across unexplored desert and braving Indian attack, the expedition ventured into the mountains and found paydirt along a stream at an elevation of 6,000 feet. A stampede of prospectors quickly ensued, giving birth to the mining camp of Ruby City.

Established in the mid-1860s, Silver City built up quickly along both sides of winding Jordan Creek.

Looking down Morning Star Street, with Silver City's impressive two-story frame schoolhouse, built in 1898, in the foreground.

When it became apparent that the location of Ruby City was exposed and windy, the population moved to a sheltered canyon about a mile upstream. The buildings, too, were hauled to the new site, and Silver City took shape on both sides of Jordan Creek.

During the next two years, more than 250 mines were begun. One of them, the War Eagle, produced $30 million worth of ore within a decade. In 1865, the fabulously rich Poorman Mine was discovered—by miners too poor to develop it. During the resulting clash over ownership, one group of claimants defiantly forted up with heavily armed gunmen and a barricade across the mine entrance.

In March of 1868, rival factions at the Golden Chariot and Ida Elmore mines skirmished for three days over their adjoining claim boundary. The usual recourse was courtroom litigation, but angry gunplay around the mine buildings produced several casualties until hostilities were halted by a cavalry detachment from Fort Boise.

Other violence occurred at the hands of Indians resentful of the mass intrusion of whites. Particularly intimidating were the depredations of a giant warrior named Nampuh (Bigfoot), who stood 6'8" and weighed 300 pounds. Nampuh's most descriptive feature, his enormous feet, were 6 inches wide and nearly eighteen inches long. Nampuh killed and robbed and terrorized throughout southern Idaho. At Fort Boise, a $1,000 reward was offered for his scalp and feet, and in 1868 he was finally slain by John Wheeler.

During the brief Bannock War of 1878, a volunteer company marched out of Silver City on June 7 to intercept the Indians. The next day, the impromptu militia was driven back with two fatalities.

By that time Silver City had enjoyed years of prosperity as one of the great bonanza sites of the West. A population of 5,000 enjoyed several theaters (Champion Hall and the Silver City Theatre were the best), a daily newspaper (the *Owyhee Avalanche*), and, beginning in 1874, one of the state's first telegraph lines.

The financial depression of the 1870s triggered a sudden population drop below 600, but in 1888, mining capitalist Joseph DeLamar purchased and vigorously developed a number of mines in the district. Despite such efforts, permanent decline had set in, and in 1935 the seat of Owyhee County, which had been moved to Silver City in 1867, was transferred to Murphy. "Old Silver" was a ghost by the 1940s.

View of Silver City as it appeared in 1907.

1. New York Summit (7,500 ft.)
2. Jordan Creek
3. Morning Star Mine
4. Knights of Pythias Cemetery
5. Owyhee County Courthouse
6. Idaho Hotel
7. *Owyhee Avalanche* Newspaper
8. Tin Shop
9. Theater
10. Masonic Hall
11. School
12. Our Lady of Tears Catholic Church
13. Corner Saloon
14. Barber Shop
15. Stoddard Mansion
16. War Eagle Saloon
17. Chinese Masonic Temple
18. Chinese Joss House
19. Chinese Cemetery

Above: Silver City street scene in the 1890s. **Opposite page:** Today, Silver City's handsome old school still hosts the annual business meeting of the Owyhee County Cattlemen's Association.

Opposite page, top: During its heyday, the 50-room Idaho Hotel promoted itself as the largest hostelry in the territory. The hotel was built in sections a mile away in Ruby City, then hauled by ox teams to Silver City, where it was hammered together in 1865. **Opposite page, bottom:** The parlor of the Idaho Hotel, overflowing with Victorian furnishings, still hosts travelers to isolated Silver City. **Above:** Silver City became the seat of Owyhee County in 1866, and an imposing courthouse and jail were built on Washington Street. The county seat was moved from the dying town in 1935, and only the stone archways of the courthouse remain, standing alongside the old drugstore.

SILVER CITY'S
CHINATOWN

Almost every Western boomtown had a Chinese section, and the 700 "celestials" of Silver City were typical in the organization of their society.

Silver City's Chinatown was clustered just across Dead Man's Alley. There were two laundries, several restaurants, five gambling halls, four stores, and two joss houses, the latter being temples where the Chinese worshiped their deities by burning incense and conducting various ceremonies.

Many of the Chinese reworked the tailings from the ore mills, or they reopened the diggings abandoned by white prospectors for richer fields. Some worked as household servants. There also were numerous Chinese woodcutters.

Until 1885, Silver City's water was provided by Chinese water carriers.

Paid 50 cents per week by each customer, they delivered 10 gallons of water daily (20 gallons on Monday washdays), loading two 5-gallon cans at a mountain spring, then carrying them into town suspended from a yoke. In 1885, the War Eagle Hotel began piping in water from nearby springs, but in winter the pipes often froze.

Many Chinese were members of "tongs," fraternal organizations that were typically headquartered in San Francisco. For an annual fee, a tong member was assisted in finding employment, provided legal aid if arrested, and assured of burial in China. By custom, the Chinese were interred with revelry and feasting, but later their remains were taken back to China—the reason why today only one body remains buried in Silver City's Chinese cemetery.

IDAHO CITY
IDAHO

Founded in 1862, Idaho City flourished and became Idaho's city of firsts. It boasted the territory's first newspaper, first Catholic church, first Masonic Hall, first Odd Fellows Hall, first store, and even the first "penitentiary" (a 20-by-24-foot log jail).

Idaho's initial discovery of gold came in the fall of 1860. This triggered intense activity by prospectors. In the summer of 1862, new gold deposits were found along the Boise River Valley, resulting in a rapid population shift to southern Idaho. Within four years, the 18-square-mile Boise Basin produced more than $24 million worth of gold.

By 1864, at least 16,000 people had swarmed into Boise Basin's mining camps. The largest community grew at the junction of Mores Creek and Elk Creek, quickly reaching a population of 6,000. The boomtown at first was called Bannock, after the Bannock Indians.

Idaho Territory's first "penitentiary" was built in May of 1864 at a cost of $10,975. Measuring 20 feet by 24 feet, the prison was built of squared, one-foot-thick logs.

Idaho City's Main Street today is still dominated by historic structures. Many tourists begin their visit at the Boise Basin Museum, located at Montgomery and Wall streets in a building that was the post office in 1864 and later housed a Wells Fargo station.

Stagecoach in front of Luna House. For 20 years, Idaho City was the largest city in the territory. Competing stagecoach lines brought large numbers of travelers to the busy center of the Boise Basin.

Soon it was learned that a Montana mining town had already taken the name of Bannack, so in 1864, Idaho's territorial legislature incorporated the Boise Basin boomtown as Idaho City.

Although Idaho City straggled for four miles along the gold-rich creeks, the business center of town was a compact quarter-mile centered around Main and Wall streets. Marion and Montgomery streets ran for half a mile parallel to Elk Creek, while most of the miners' cabins were scattered across the land rising up behind the creeks.

Writing in 1980, historian Hubert Howe Bancroft obtained the following description of Idaho City in its heyday: "There were 250 places of business, well-filled stores, highly decorated and resplendent gambling saloons, a hospital for sick and indigent miners, Protestant and Catholic churches, a theatre, three newspapers, and a fire department."

But the fire department proved inadequate. On the night of May 18, 1865, fire broke out in the upper story of a hurdy-gurdy house. Fanned by a strong wind, the blaze raged uncontrolled until four-fifths of the city was destroyed. The new Forrest Theatre, open for only its second night, was burned to the ground, along with all but 20 or 30 businesses. Within two months, however, the thriving city was rebuilt.

Resident Charles Teeter wrote to his sister: "Drinking saloons, gambling houses, dry goods establishments, barber shops, and everything else have opened in grander style, and upon a larger scale than before."

Fire struck again in 1867, 1868, and 1871, but Idaho City bounced back each time with frontier resiliency. A kiln on Elk Creek provided bricks for rebuilding, and many of the masonry structures still stand. Some of them housed the nearly two dozen law offices that busily litigated the conflicting claims common to mining districts.

There were 46 saloons, supplied in part by four breweries. A saloon fiddler named Kelley became so frightened over the relentlessly rowdy atmosphere that he played on a specially built platform suspended by a system of ropes and pulleys from the ceiling; when gunfire erupted, he was hauled upward, gamely continuing to work his instrument out of harm's way.

The most troublesome lawlessness occurred not in the saloons but on the roads connecting Idaho City with Centerville, Comeback, Golden Age, Placerville, Granite, Pioneerville, Quartzburg, and other towns of the district, as well as more distant communities. Teddy White and other highwaymen robbed stagecoaches, express hacks, and freight wagons with such frequency that even Wells Fargo temporarily suspended operations.

The district was tame by the 1870s, when declining production and new strikes in other areas triggered the inevitable exodus. In 1898, dredging operations temporarily revived Idaho City, but the census of 1920 revealed a population of only 104.

Today, historic Idaho City boasts a fine museum and so many venerable buildings that it exerts a magnetic pull upon ghost town buffs.

Interior of Idaho City's Boise Basin Mercantile. The date of the photo is unknown, but the building was constructed in 1865 and still stands as Idaho's oldest existing store.

Main Street during the late 19th century. At the center of the photo is a blacksmith shop, and next to it is a building that housed the *Idaho World* newspaper for a time.

Upper left: Diamond Lil's Saloon. **Left:** Happy Burr Trading Post on Main Street.
Above: Exterior of the old schoolhouse. Ghost town buffs and tourists alike will find
plenty of diversions in Idaho City.

Inside the old schoolhouse is Jean Stover Antiques. Many of the town's original structures have been restored to serve visitors.

Upper left: Ore car. By 1866, the Boise Basin mines had produced $24 million in gold. **Above:** Idaho City firehouse. Local firefighters had to battle major blazes in 1865, 1867, 1868, and 1871. **Left:** Hose rigs like this one in the Idaho City firehouse were essential in fighting the fires that plagued ramshackle mining towns throughout the West.

ST. JOSEPH'S
CATHOLIC CHURCH

Among the thousands of inhabitants of Idaho City were a number of women, children, and family men who preferred to spend Sundays in a church rather than in a saloon or brothel.

Several denominational groups—including Catholics, Baptists, and Methodists—met in members' homes until they were able to build churches. As it turned out, the first church in Idaho City was St. Joseph's, which also had the distinction of being the first Catholic church in Idaho.

Catholic missionaries to the Indians were assigned to the Northwest as early as 1838, and there were numerous converts by the early 1860s, when the mining boom brought large numbers of Irish Catholics into Idaho.

Fathers Toussaint Mesplie and Andre Poulin were sent from Oregon to Idaho City in 1864, and sufficient funds were collected by the priests to purchase land on East Hill. Religious services were held in a downtown residence while a suitable frame structure measuring 20 feet by 75 feet was erected on the site. The church was dedicated on November 15, 1863.

St. Joseph's Church was consumed in the fire of 1867. Before the end of that year, however, the priests had gathered the resources to rebuild it. Soon, four nuns arrived and established St. Mary's Academy for girls, which operated for eight years, until Idaho City's population decline reduced attendance at the school.

The last resident priest was Father James Thomas, who assumed his duties in 1898. Three years later Father Thomas was transferred, and St. Joseph's was reduced to mission status. But area priests have continued to travel to Idaho City to conduct services at the church, which is maintained as one of the handsomest buildings of the old mining town.

Opened in 1863, St. Joseph's was the first church in Idaho City and the first Catholic church in the territory. The original building was destroyed in the fire of 1867, but was rebuilt the following year.

PORT BLAKELY
WASHINGTON

The Western frontier communities that most readily come to mind are mining or cattle towns, but logging was a pioneer industry as well. Port Blakely, Washington, provides an excellent example of a ghost from the timber industry, though little remains of the site.

Logging on the West Coast was only a sporadic enterprise until the California gold rush created a voracious market for lumber. As demands for wood soared, crews entered the enormous Western timber stands, and sawmills operated continuously.

During the 1850s, mills began to appear on Puget Sound, which featured a protected coastline, and thanks to the warming effects of the Japanese current, enjoyed an ice-free climate year round. In 1863, William Renton built the Port Blakely Mill on the southeastern shore of Bainbridge Island. A partner, Charles S. Holmes, supervised marketing activities from

A tugboat is moored near the former site of the Hall Brothers Shipyard, which built 50 lumber-carrying ships between 1880 and 1903, plus three 484-ton sternwheelers for the Yukon River trade.

These rotting pilings are all that remain of the once extensive wharves of Port Blakely.

Right: Ships under construction in Port Blakely Harbor. **Below:** The Hall Brothers Shipyard was located in Port Ludlow in the 1870s. It moved to Port Blakely in the 1880s, then to Eagle Harbor in the 1890s.

Large timbers bound for England are loaded onto an oceangoing ship at the Port Blakely Mill.

an office in San Francisco, and orders became so extensive that the mill was expanded.

It soon was obvious that the timber supply of Bainbridge Island would become exhausted. Sol Simpson, an experienced railroad builder from Nevada, was brought in, and he acquired a local line, the Puget Sound & Grays Harbor. Changing the name to the G. S. Simpson Co., he extended the line to Port Blakely and to several other area mills, and the railroad became known as the Blakely Line.

Despite two destructive fires, the mill was rebuilt and enlarged. After Edison invented the light bulb in 1879, night shifts became possible, and the giant saw operated around the clock.

A log pond was essential for holding timber until it could be milled, so a dam with sturdy flood gates was constructed across the opening to a conveniently located inlet.

In 1883, the Northern Pacific was completed, providing a rail connection with Eastern markets. By 1885, the Port Blakely Mill was the world's largest, employing 1,200 men.

With his mill cutting 400,000 feet of lumber per day, Renton acquired 80,000 acres of standing timber on the mainland. Another acquisition was the Russian gunboat *Politokofsky,* turned over to the U. S. government as part of the Alaska purchase of 1867 and bought by the Port Blakely Mill Company at a government surplus sale. The guns were removed, and the ship was used as a carrier around Puget Sound.

Renton's company also purchased five lumber schooners as carriers, as well as a tugboat used to shove logs around the Sound. When the Hall Brothers Shipyard was constructed near the Port Blakely Mill in 1881, the S.S. *Julia*—the largest sternwheeler in the Northwest—was built, along with scores of schooners and other craft.

With a hill rising close beyond the shoreline, the town of Port Blakely was narrow, constructed around a single long street that was littered with tree stumps. A two-story hotel faced the bay, with a big front porch connected to the wharf where passenger ships unloaded. There were saloons and stores, as well as a school and post office.

The shipyard closed in 1903, and changing conditions in the timber industry caused the mill to shut down shortly after the close of World War I. The mill buildings were dismantled and removed, and the town of Port Blakely quickly shriveled to ghost town status.

Today, all that remains of the old lumber town are its building foundations, remnants of the log pond dam, and the broken stubs of pilings.

Opposite page, top: Port Blakely around the turn of the century. The town was long and narrow, lining the waterfront. The railroad line served the Hall Brothers Shipyard. In the background, partially obscured by trees, is a two-story hotel. Note also the photographer's tent in the foreground.
Opposite page, bottom: A few homes from the late 1800s have survived, although most have been extensively remodeled over the years.

Right: Tombstone of a native of Finland. The Port Blakely cemetery is nestled in the woods approximately half a mile north of the harbor. Other ethnic groups represented here include Japanese, Hawaiians, Swedes, and Norwegians. **Far right:** Note the Latin inscription on this tombstone monument. The Internal Order of Woodsmen promised each of its members a tombstone at death.

Below: A moderate telephoto lens shows the northern edge of the harbor, at left, and its location in relation to the Seattle skyline.

A SLANG OF THEIR OWN
LOGGERS' LINGO

The language of the logging frontier was as colorful as the *timber beasts, sawdust savages, log jockeys, bush rats,* and *lumber rustlers* who attacked the vast timber stands of the West.

River pigs conducted *river drives,* herding as many as 10 million feet of logs downstream and receiving top wages because they were wet all the time. A *ball hooter* rolled logs down a hillside, a *donkey doctor* maintained and repaired portable steam engines *(steam donkeys)* used in cable loggings, and a *bull of the woods* was foreman of a logging camp.

The *deacon seat* was a plank or split-log bunkhouse bench placed in front of the bunks, and a *muzzle loader* was a bunkhouse so crowded that timber beasts had to climb into their bunks from the foot of the bed rather than the side.

Sawdust savages wore *tin pants,* heavy canvas breeches that were waterproofed. A *faller* cut the trees, beginning with a *cow's mouth,* the falling notch he fashioned. And various items of equipment were known as a *Swede fiddle, picaroon, iron mule, bitch chain, gut wrapper, hoot-nanny,* and *Irish baby buggy.* Additional items were known by terms too vulgar to mention here.

When this photo was taken, during the winter of 1910, Port Blakely was already in decline. Before another decade would pass, the mills would be closed forever.

JACKSONVILLE
OREGON

Pioneer farmers and their families had been streaming into Oregon along the Oregon Trail since the early 1840s, but the gold rush to California was far more spectacular.

That situation changed somewhat in December of 1851, when a pair of mule packers en route from Portland, Oregon, to Yreka, California, accidentally discovered gold near their campsite at Daisy Creek. By the next summer, prospectors were swarming into Oregon.

Where Daisy Creek met Jackson Creek, a mining camp boomed into Jacksonville, Oregon's largest town (though Portland was still the territory's premier city). Jacksonville became the seat of Jackson County in 1853, and the population soon reached an estimated 15,000. There was revelry and violence typical of raw mining towns, but the early presence of county governmental institutions

Ten miles outside of Jacksonville is the picturesque McKee Bridge, built in 1917 over the Applegate River. The bridge was named after Dee McKee, whose home served as a stagecoach station between Jacksonville and the Blue Ledge Copper Mine.

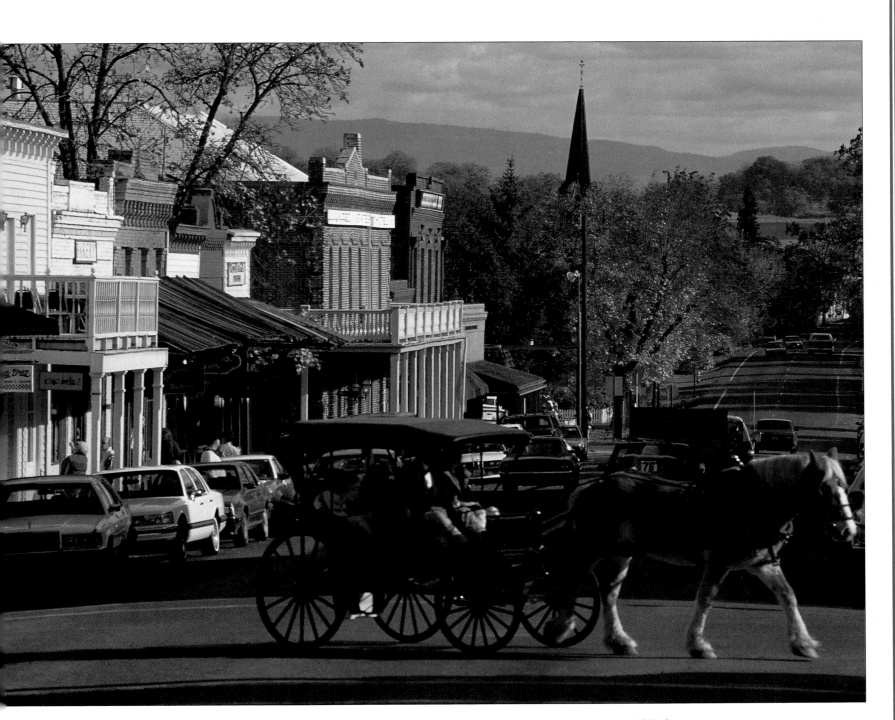

A boomtown called Table Rock City quickly sprang up near the site of a gold discovery in southern Oregon in 1851. Soon renamed Jacksonville, the town served as the center of the region's commercial activities until it was bypassed by the Oregon & California Railroad in 1884. Today, Jacksonville boasts some of the most interesting historic architecture in the Pacific Northwest.

Jacksonville carpenter and cabinet maker David Linn built this attractive Victorian Gothic Presbyterian Church, completed in 1881. Town banker C. C. Beekman donated the 1,000-pound bell, purchased in San Francisco, and also contributed nearly half of the construction cost.

was a strong civilizing influence. Jacksonville was plagued by other problems, however.

Oregon's Rogue River War of 1855-56 was the most serious of several early Indian scares, temporarily halting mining activity. In 1868, a small-pox epidemic ravaged Jacksonville's population, removing several key civic leaders. The next year the creeks overflowed and filled Jacksonville with tons of mud and gravel. Having survived all of that, the town was seriously damaged by fire in 1874 and again in 1875.

Following every crisis, the citizens of Jacksonville rebounded resolutely, and a hand-some frontier community developed. During the 1850s, brick commercial structures began to go up on California and Oregon streets, and Victorian residences were built on avenues comfort-ably shaded by trees.

Although gold production dropped off in the 1860s and the population began to decline, Jacksonville rallied as a trade center for the bur-geoning agricultural activity of the fertile Rogue River Valley.

In 1880, President Rutherford B. Hayes came to town, staying in the new United States Hotel. A fine courthouse was erected in 1883, but the next year Jacksonville was bypassed by the Oregon & California Railroad. Tracks were laid through Medford, five miles to the east, and the farm trade gravitated there. In 1927, with Jacksonville's population down to 1,500, the county seat was moved to Medford as well.

In 1950, Jacksonville began yet another come-back, capitalizing on its history and attractive set-ting to become a genuine tourist attraction.

P. BRITT, PHOTO

Above: Fourth of July parade in Jacksonville during the 1870s. In frontier towns, the Fourth of July was always celebrated with enthusiasm. **Right:** The Jacksonville Inn is located on California Street in the center of historic Jacksonville. Built in 1863, it is one of Jacksonville's earliest structures, yet continues to provide quality accommodations. The restaurant is nationally acclaimed, and the Wine and Gift Shop features 700 fine wines. To the left of the Jacksonville Inn is the U.S. Hotel, built in 1880.

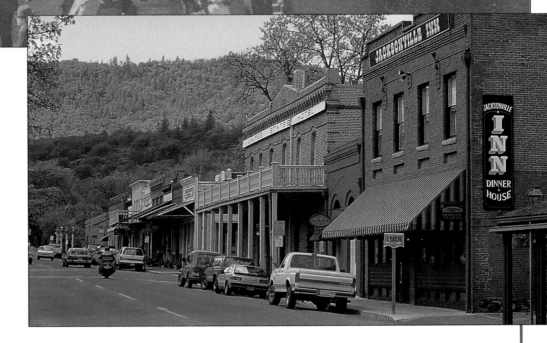

Below: Early settlers clashed with the Indians. In one recorded incident, a certain Mrs. Harris survived a harrowing experience, single-handedly defending her family's farm, located on the outskirts of Jacksonville, from Indian attack. After her husband George was mortally wounded during the initial assault, Mrs. Harris dragged him inside their cabin, barring the door and instructing her daughter to hide in the loft. For five hours she kept the Indians at bay by firing shotgun blasts at them from different windows throughout the house, apparently convincing them that the building was being defended by several men. Growing impatient with the standoff—and eager to fulfill their mission of revenge for atrocities committed against their people—the war party withdrew to a neighboring farm, where they killed a family of four.

Opposite page, top left: The Methodist Church, built in 1854, was Jacksonville's first house of worship and the first Protestant church west of the Rockies. Generous contributions to the construction fund were made by miners, most of whom came into town for less sacred pursuits. The old church now is home to St. Andrew's Episcopal congregation.

Opposite page, bottom: Erected in 1892, the Jeremiah Nunan House is often called the "Catalog House." A wealthy merchant, Nunan ordered his home from the George F. Barber Cottage Souvenir Catalog. Completed in less than six months at a cost of $7,800, the house was a Christmas gift for his wife, Deilia. **Above:** This early but undated view of Jacksonville shows the Jackson County Courthouse, built in 1883, to the right of center near the top of photo, and, to the left of center, the town's Catholic Church, built in 1858.

BRINGING A GHOST
BACK TO LIFE

Because the town of Medford, five miles away, absorbed most of the growth of the region, Jacksonville's historic buildings did not have to be razed to make way for new construction.

In 1950, the citizens of Jacksonville restored the 1883 courthouse and turned it into a museum.

A few old structures re-opened as antique shops, and some of the venerable residences became bed-and-breakfasts.

A leading citizen of early Jacksonville, banker Cornelius C. Beekman built a fine home in 1875, and today visitors are escorted through the Beekman House by guides attired in period dress. The Beekman Bank, built in 1863, also welcomes tourists, and the old jail is the home of a fine hands-on children's museum of pioneer artifacts.

Among 80 brick and frame structures scattered through two dozen blocks of Jacksonville, perhaps 40 have been restored, and the town has been designated a National Historic Landmark.

Below left: Originally the Jackson County Courthouse, this handsome Italianate-style structure, built in 1883, today is home to the Jacksonville Museum of Southern Oregon History. **Below:** The Beekman House, constructed in 1880 for Jacksonville banker C. C. Beekman, is the setting for living history tours each summer, when members of the Southern Oregon Historical Society portray local citizens and servants as they might have been in the year 1911.

Above: White-bearded C. C. Beekman, banker and civic leader, in his bank with one of his employees. The Beekman Bank was constructed in 1862 on the corner of California and Third streets.

Right: One of Jacksonville's oldest buildings, the Beekman Bank today appears pretty much as it did during the 19th century.

309

Index

American Smelting and Refining Company (Silverbell, Arizona), 178
Arizona Rangers, 176
Arizona Southern Railroad, 176, *176*, 177
Army, United States, 86
  scouts, 21
  7th Cavalry, 12
Atchison, Topeka & Santa Fe Railroad, 34
Bainbridge Island, 294, 298
Bannock War, 278
Bass, Sam, 16
Battle of Ingalls, 48–49
Battle of Round Mountains, 52
Beekman, Cornelius C., 304, 308, 309, *309*
Bennett, Horace, 84
Big Casino (Tonopah, Nevada), 224, 226, *226*, 227, *227*
"The Big Fight" (Tascosa, Texas), 63
"The Big House" (Lincoln, New Mexico), 200, 200, 201, 202, 209, *209*
Billy the Kid, 35, 41, 54, 56, 192, 201, 202, 206, 206, 207, *207*, 209
Bird Cage Theatre (Tombstone, Arizona), 164, 173, *173*
"Bisbee Massacre," 166
Bivins, Julian, 55, 58, 62
Black Hills Expedition, 14
Blake, Tulsa Jack, 48, 49
Blakely Line, 298
Bodey, Bill, 256, 258
Bodie Railway and Lumber Company (Bodie, California), 260
Bonny, William. *See* Billy the Kid
Bovey, Charles and Sue, 146, 147
Boys Ranch (Texas), 58, 59, *59*, 62, *62*
Bozeman Trail, 149
Brady, Jim, 68
Brady, Matthew, 14
Brady, William, 200, 201, 207
Breakenridge, Billy, 165
Brocius, Curly Bill, 166
Brown, George, 32
Brown, Henry, 35, 41, *41*, 54
Brown, W.D., 182
Bryant, Frank, 14
Bucket of Blood Saloon (Virginia City, Nevada), 220, 221
Buckley, William, 249
Buffalo, 30, 41, 54, 66
Bulette, Julia, 217
Bull whacking, 23
Burke, Charley, 23
Burlesque, 108, 173
Burnett, Reuben, 176
Butch Cassidy and the Sundance Kid (film), 250, 252

Butler, Belle, 222, 225, *225*
Butler, "Lazy Jim," 222, 224, *224*, 225, *225*
Butterfield Stagecoach, 182
Calamity Jane, 16, 23, 23, 116
California Rangers, 273
Call, W. R., 46
Cannary, Martha Jane, 23, *23*
Carlyle, Jim, 192
Cassidy, Butch, 134, *134*, 135
"Catalog House" (Jacksonville, Oregon), 306, 307
Cattle drives, 16, 17, 34, 149
Cattle ranges, 84
Cemeteries
  Aurora, Nevada, 248, *248*
  Bannack, Montana, 158, *158*
  Boot Hill (Tascosa, Texas), 54, 56, 58, 65, *65*
  Boot Hill (Tombstone, Arizona), 162, *162*, 166
  Boot Hill (Virginia City, Montana), 144, *144*
  Creede, Colorado, 120
  Grafton, Utah, 252
  Hornitos, California, 271, *271*
  Mobeetie, Texas, 72
  Mt. Moriah (Deadwood, South Dakota), 21, 22
  Port Blakely, Washington, 300, *300*
  Shakespeare, New Mexico, 184, 189, *189*
  Shotgun Hill (Creede, Colorado), 120, *120*
  Silverbell, Arizona, 178, 179
  Terlingua, Texas, 80, *80*
Central City Opera House (Central City, Colorado), 110, 111
Chateau de Mores (Medora, North Dakota), 25, 25, 26, 27
Cherokee Strip, 36, 38, *38*
Chinese immigrants, 14, 35, 108, 110, 260, 270, 283
Chisholm, James, 128
Chisholm Trail, 32, 36, 42, 43
Chisos Mining Company (Texas), 76, 81
Chisum, John, 54, 200, 201, *201*
Civil War, 21, 53, 246
Claiborne, Billy, 166, 172
Clanton, Billy, 165, 165, 170
Clanton-McLaury gang, 164, 170
Clemens, Orion, 247
Clemens, Samuel. *See* Twain, Mark
Cleveland, Jack, 152
Clifton, Dynamite Dick, 48, 49
Colorado Central Railroad, 114
Comstock, Henry, 212
Comstock Lode, 182, 210, 212, 214, 219, 225
Continental Divide, 96, 126
Copper, 18, 96, 174, 176, 180, 302
Courthouses
  Bannack, Montana, 154, 155, *155*
  Jacksonville, Oregon, 304, 307, *307*, 308, *308*

Mobeetie, Texas, 68, *68*
Silver City, Idaho, 283, *283*
Tascosa, Texas, 58, 59, *59*
Tascosa, ts, 55, *55*
Tombstone, Arizona, 164, 168, *168*
Tonopah, Nevada, 225
Virginia City, Montana, 141, *141*, 144
Virginia City, Nevada, 214
Wheeler County (Texas), 70, *70*
Cowboys, 30, 35, 36, 39, 41, 50, 51, *51*, 56, 60, 60, 61, *61*, 63, 73, 74, 132, 149, 237
Creede, Nicholas C., 118, *118*
Creede Candle (newspaper), 116
Creede Opera House (Colorado), 122, *122*
Crime, 16, 50, 135, 142, 150, 152, 260, 267, 287
Cripple Creek Railroad (Colorado), 94
Crystal Palace Saloon (Tombstone, Arizona), 163, *163*, 164, 166, 167, 167, 168, 169
Custer, George Armstrong, 12, 14
Dalton, Bill, 48, 49
Dalton gang, 50
DeLamar, Joseph, 278
Denver and Rio Grande Railroad, 98, 119
Denver Exchange Saloon (Creede, Colorado), 125
DeRoche, Joseph, 267
Doolin, Bill, 44, 47, 48, 49, 50, *50*, 51
Dumont, Eleanor, 164
Earp, James, 165
Earp, Morgan, 16, 165, *165*, 170
Earp, Virgil, 163, 165, *165*, 170
Earp, Wyatt, 16, 165, *165*, 170
Elkhorn Ranch (Medora, North Dakota), 30, 31
Ellsworth, J. W., 46
Emory, Charley, 63
Equity Bar (Tascosa, Texas), 56, 57, *57*
Esmerelda Rangers, 246
Evenson, "Uncle Johnny," 182
Fairweather, William H., 140, 145, *145*
Fairweather Inn (Virginia City, Montana), 145, *145*
Farley, Cal, 58, 59, 62
Fires
  Bodie, California, 256, 258
  Caldwell, Kansas, 35
  Central City, Colorado, 110
  Creede, Colorado, 120
  Cripple Creek, Colorado, 86, 88, 89, 95
  Deadwood, South Dakota, 16
  Goldfield, Nevada, 238
  Idaho City, Idaho, 287, 292
  Medora, North Dakota, 29
  Silverbell, Arizona, 177
  Tombstone, Arizona, 162, 167, 167
  Virginia City, Nevada, 212, 214, 215
  White Oaks, New Mexico, 192

Fisher, Big Nose Kate, 164
Flatt, George, 32
Floods
    Deadwood, South Dakota, 16
    Grafton, Utah, 252, 255
    Jacksonville, Oregon, 304
    Tascosa, Texas, 56
Ford, Bob, 120
Ford, Pat, 158
Fort Boise, 278
Fort Elliott, 66, 68, *68*, 69
Fort Fred Steele, 134
Fort Phil Kearny, 149
Fort Reno, 149
Fort Smith, 149
Fort Stanton, 192, 201
Fort Sumner, 207
Frontier towns
    Caldwell, Kansas, 32–43
    Deadwood, South Dakota, 12–23
    Medora, North Dakota, 24–29
    Mobeetie, Texas, 66–73
Gambling, 16, 20, 21, 47, 54, 56, 66, 90, 96, 98,
    113, 116, 118, 125, 128, 142, 158, 164, 173,
    190, 234, 237, 283, 287
Gans, Joe, 237
Garrett, Pat, 54, 56, 202, 206, *206*, 207, 209
Ghirardelli, D., 271
"Ghost of Sonora," 273
Gold, 12, 14, 84, 90, 93, 96, 106, 120, 126, 127,
    142, 150, 153, 190, 212, 219, 222, 234, 240,
    241, 246, 256, 258, 262, 268, 273, 276, 302
Goldfield Hotel (Goldfield, Nevada), 234, *234*,
    237, 238
Grand Opera House (Cripple Creek, Colorado),
    90
Grant, Ulysses S., 114
Grant House (Shakespeare, New Mexico), 182,
    182, 183, *183*, 184, 185, 187, *187*, 188, 189
Graves, Fielding L., 152, 159
Graves, Robert N., 218
Greathouse, Jim, 192
Greeley, Horace, 106, 108, *108*
Gregory, John H., 106
G. S. Simpson Company (Port Blakely,
    Washington), 298
Gunfighters, 36, 39, 54, 56, 125
Gunfights, 49, 99, 164, 166, 170, 201, 260
Hall Brothers Shipyard (Port Blakely,
    Washington), 294, *294*, 296, *296*, 298, 299
Harte, Bret, 270
Hayes, Rutherford B., 304
Heath, John, 166, 166
Helldorado Festival, 165, *165*
Helm, Boone, 142
Hewitt, John Y., 195
Hickock, Wild Bill, 14, 16, 21, *21*, 23
Hill, Frank, 185
Hill, Janaloo, 185
Holliday, Doc, 98, 99, *99*, 164, 168, 170
"Home Rangers," 56
Homesteaders, 34, 36, 38, 44, 47

Hornitos Hotel (Hornitos, California), 271
Horrell War, 200
Hotel Chisos (Terlingua, Texas), 76, 77
Houston, Temple, 54, 66, 68, 69, 73, *73*
Hoyle, Watson, 197
Hoyle Castle (White Oaks, New Mexico), 196,
    197
Hueston, Tom, 48
Hughes, Howard, 226
Idaho Hotel (Silver City, Idaho), 282, 283
Imperial Copper Company (Silverbell, Arizona),
    176, 177
Indians
    Apaches, 74, 162, 185, *185*, 186, 198
    attacks by, 12, 128, 134, 149, 252, 258, 278,
      304, 307
    Bannock, 284
    Comanches, 54, 74
    Five Civilized Tribes, 52
    Kiowas, 54
    legends, 12
    Paiute, 258
    Shawnees, 74
    Shoshone, 222
    Sioux, 12
Indian Territory, 50, 52
Indian wars, 21
Jacksonville Inn (Jacksonville, Oregon), 305, 305
James, Jesse, 120
Jenkins and Dunn Saloon (Tascosa, Texas), 63,
    63
Johnson, Turkey Creek Jack, 16
Jones, Arkansas Tom, 48, 49
Jordan, Michael, 276
Joss houses, 283
Kelly, Ed O., 120
Kid Curry, 134, *134*
King, Sandy, 184, 187, 189
Kuykendall Transportation Company, 88
Land rushes, 34, 36, 44
Lawmen, 16, 32, 41, 44, 48, 56, 63, 86, 90, 176,
    187, 192, 198, 201, 202, 237
Leland Hotel (Caldwell, Kansas), 35
Leslie, Buckskin Frank, 166, 172
Lincoln County War, 41, 56, 200, 201, 207, 209
Logan, Harvey, 16, 134, *134*
Logging towns, 294–301
Longabaugh, Harry, 134, *134*
Lucky Cuss Saloon (Tombstone, Arizona), 170,
    171
Lumberjacks, 134
Lynching, 41, 86, 142, 144, 154, 166, 184, 189,
    192, 267
McCall, Jack, 16, 21
McCormick, Frenchy, 58, *58*
McCormick, Mickey, 58
McDowell, "Three-Fingered Jack," 249
McEven, Sam, 176
McLaury, Frank, 165, *165*, 170
McLaury, Tom, 165, *165*, 170
McMurtry, Robert F., 44, 46
McSween, Alexander, 200, 201, *201*

Maltese Cross Ranch (Medora, North Dakota),
    30, 31
Marsh, Billy, 234
Masterson, Bat, 69, 98, 116, 125, *125*
Meade Hotel (Bannack, Montana), 154, 155, *155*
Meyers, Julian, 84
Mignon, Joe, 164
Millain, John, 217
Mines
    Atwood (Shakespeare, New Mexico), 184, 185
    Belcher (Virginia City, Nevada), 212
    Black Prince (White Oaks, New Mexico), 194
    Bunker Hill (Bodie, California), 258
    California (Virginia City, Nevada), 212
    Captain Kidd (White Oaks, New Mexico), 194
    Carissa (South Pass City, Wyoming), 127, 128
    Climax Molybdenum (Leadville, Colorado),
      104, *104*
    Commodore (Creede, Colorado), 121, *121*
    Comstock (White Oaks, New Mexico), 194
    Discovery (White Oaks, New Mexico), 194
    Gould & Curry (Virginia City, Nevada), 212,
      214
    Graveyard (Tombstone, Arizona), 162
    Henry Clay (Shakespeare, New Mexico), 184,
      185, 194
    Homestake Mine (Deadwood, South Dakota),
      16
    Jenny Lind (Hornitos, California), 268
    Little Jonny (Leadville, Colorado), 99
    Little Mack (White Oaks, New Mexico), 194
    Little Nell (White Oaks, New Mexico), 194
    Little Pittsburg (Leadville, Colorado), 104,
      104
    Lucky Cuss (Tombstone, Arizona), 162
    Mammoth (Silverbell, Arizona), 177
    Matchless (Leadville, Colorado), 104
    Mizpah (Tonopah, Nevada), 224
    Mohawk (Goldfield, Nevada), 241
    North Homestake (White Oaks, New Mexico),
      192, 194, *194*
    Old Abe (White Oaks, New Mexico), 192, 193,
      193, 194
    Rip Van Winkle (White Oaks, New Mexico),
      194
    Robert E. Lee (Leadville, Colorado), 98, 104,
      104
    Ruth Pierce (Hornitos, California), 268
    South Homestake (White Oaks, New Mexico),
      192, 194
    Toughnut (Tombstone, Arizona), 162
    War Eagle (Silver City, Idaho), 278
    Yellow Jacket (Shakespeare, New Mexico),
      184
Mining towns
    Aurora, Nevada, 244–249
    Bannack, Montana, 150–159
    Bodie, California, 256–267
    Central City, Colorado, 106–115
    Creede, Colorado, 116–125
    Cripple Creek, Colorado, 84–95
    Deadwood, South Dakota, 12–23

Goldfield, Nevada, 234–243
Grandpa, Nevada, 234
Hornitos, California, 268–273
Idaho City, Idaho, 284–293
Independence (Cripple Creek, Colorado), 95
Jacksonville, Oregon, 302–309
Leadville, Colorado, 96–105
Little Pittsburg (Leadville, Colorado), 100
Shakespeare, New Mexico, 182–189
Silverbell, Arizona, 174–180
Silver City, Idaho, 276–283
Southern Klondike (Nevada), 222
South Pass City, Wyoming, 126–131
Tombstone, Arizona, 162–173
Tonopah, Nevada, 222–233
Virginia City, Montana, 140–149
Virginia City, Nevada, 210–221
White Oaks, New Mexico, 190
Mizpah Hotel (Tonopah, Nevada), 227, *227*, 230, *230*, 231, *231*
Mizpah Saloon & Grill (Tonopah, Nevada), 230
Montana Hotel (Bannack, Montana), 151, *151*
Mores, Marquis de, 24, 26, 27
Mormons, 250, 252
Morris, Esther, 131
Murieta, Joaquin, 270, 273
Murphy, Lawrence G., 200, 209
Nampuh (Indian warrior), 278
Nation, Carry, 90
National Hotel (Cripple Creek, Colorado), 90
Newcomb, Bitter Creek, 48
Northern Pacific Railroad, 26, 298
Northern Saloon (Aurora, Nevada), 247
Nye, James W., 249
Oddie, Tasker, 224, 228, *228*
O.K. Corral, 164, 166, 170
O.K. Hotel (Ingalls, Oklahoma), 47, 48, *48*
"Oklahombres," 44, 50
Olinger, Bob, 207
Opera House (Caldwell, Kansas), 35, *35*, 37, *37*
Opium dens, 142, 260, 270
Oregon Trail, 302
Oriental Saloon (Tombstone, Arizona), 164, 166, 168, 172, *172*
Outlaws, 44, 54, 56, 174, 192, 198, 249, 287
Owyhee Avalanche (newspaper), 278
Palace Hotel (Creede, Colorado), 119
Parish, Frank, 144
Parker, Jess, 74
Parker, Morris, 192
Parker, Robert Leroy, 134, *134*
Perry, Howard, 75, 76, 81
Picacho Mining company (Silverbell, Arizona), 181
Pickering, Jacob, 46
Piper's Opera House (Virginia City, Nevada), 214, 215, *215*
Plummer, George, 136
Plummer, Henry, 150, 154, 158
Port Blakely Mill (Port Blakely, Washington), 294, 297, *297*, 298
Posses, 135, 267

Prostitution, 39, 47, 56, 63, 66, 68, 90, 94, 96, 98, 116, 118, 128, 142, 164, 173, 184, 190, 192, 214, 217, 234, 246, 260, 270
Quicksilver, 76, 81
Railroads, 34, 36, 49, 89, 95, 108, 192, 225, 226, 298
Ray, Ned, 152, 154
Red Garter Saloon (Virginia City, Nevada), 211, *211*
Red Light Saloon (Caldwell, Kansas), 32
"Regulators," 201, 207
Renton, William, 294
Rickard, George Lewis "Tex," 237, 238
Ringo, John, 166
"Road Agents," 150, 154
Rogue River War, 304
Roosevelt, Theodore, 26, 29, 30, *30*, 31, 94, *94*, 139
Rudabaugh, Dave, 192
Russell, Charles, 134
Russian Bill, 184, 187, 189
Rustling, 41, 56, 60, 170, 184, 187, 200, 249
Sacramento Union (newspaper), 260
Saloons, 14, 34, 35, 46, 47, 54, 67, *67*, 68, 69, 96, 98, 142, 144
Schieffelin, Ed, 162, 170
Shadley, Lafe, 48
Shakespeare Mining Company (Shakespeare, New Mexico), 184
Sherlock Hotel (South Pass City, Wyoming), 129, *129*, 130, *130*
Short, Luke, 98, 99, *99*, 172
Silver, 96, 100, 118, 120, 162, 182, 210, 219, 246, 276
Silver Queen Saloon (Virginia City, Nevada), 216, *216*
Simpson, Sol, 298
Slade, Jack, 144
Smith, Jefferson Randolph "Soapy," 116, 121, *121*, 125
Southern Arizona Smelting Company (Silverbell, Arizona), 177, 181
Southern Pacific Railroad, 185
Southwestern Hotel (Caldwell, Kansas), 35
Speed, Dick, 48, 49
Stagecoaches, 88, *88*, 150, 184, 267, 286, *286*, 287
Stamp mills, 244, *244*, 246, 247, 268
Stevens, Will, 96
Stimler, Harry, 234
Stinson, Buck, 152, 154
Story, Nelson, 149
Stratford Hotel (Shakespeare, New Mexico), 184
Stratton, Winfield Scott, 95, *95*
Street, Julian, 90
"Suicide Table" (Delta Saloon), 220
Sundance Kid, 134, *134*
Tabor, Augusta Pierce, 100, *100*
Tabor, Baby Doe, 100, *100*
Tabor, H.A.W., 98, 99, 100, *100*, 114
Tabor Grand Hotel (Leadville, Colorado), 98, 99, *99*

Tabor Opera House (Leadville, Colorado), 98, 101, *101*
Telegraph, 14, 192
Teller, Henry M., 114
Teller House (Central City, Colorado), 114, *114*, 115, *115*
Tenney, Marvelous Flood, 255
Tenney, Nathan, 255
Territorial Enterprise (newspaper), 216
Tethenborn, Waldemar. *See* Russian Bill
Thomas, Heck, 50, *50*
Thompson, Ben, 98
Tilghman, Bill, 50, *50*
Tombstone Epitaph (newspaper), 164, 168
Tombstone Prospector (newspaper), 168
Tonopah Mining Company (Tonopah, Nevada), 224
Tourism, 16, 19, 20, 21, 26, 90, 91, 94, 97, 98, 101, 105, 120, 122, 123, 148, 165, 166, 172, 185, 214, 219, 226, 238, 285, 304, 308
Tubbs, Poker Alice, 116, 121, *121*
Tunstall, John, 200, 201, *201*, 207
Twain, Mark, 210, 214, 216, *216*, 247, *247*, 258, 260
Union Pacific Railroad, 43, 128, 132, 133, 134, 135
United States Hotel (Jacksonville, Oregon), 304, 305, *305*
Vallombrosa, Antoine Amedee Marie Vincent Amat Manca de. *See* Mores, Marquis de
Victorio (Apache chief), 185, *185*
Vigilantes, 142, 184, 200, 249, 270
Violence, 32, 35, 39, 41, 63, 164, 198, 302, 304, 307
Virginian Hotel (Medicine Bow, Wyoming), 134, 132, *132*, 136, *136*, 137, *137*
Virginian, The (book), 134, 139
Virginia & Truckee Railroad, 219, *219*
von Hoffman, Medora, 24, 25, 27
Waightman, Red Buck, 48
Wallace, Lew, 206, 207
War Eagle Hotel (Silver City, Idaho), 283
Wheeler, Ben, 41
Wheeler, John, 278
White, Fred, 166
White, John, 150
White, Teddy, 287
Whitehill, Harvey, 187
White House Saloon (Cripple Creek, Colorado), 87
White Oaks Eagle (newspaper), 195
The Wild Bunch, 16, 134, *134*, 135, 170
Wild West Shows, 21, 23
Wister, Owen, 134, 136, 138, 139, *139*
Woodruff, Lem, 63
Wortley Hotel (Lincoln, New Mexico), 200, *200*, 205, *205*
Young, Brigham, 252
Zion National Park, 252, 254, *254*